£3.55

Printed and Published in Great Britain by D. C. THOMSON & CO., LTD., 185 Fleet Street, London EC4A 2HS.

ISBN 0 85116 476 5

25 ways to notice

1. Dress yourself up in a totally outrageous dress and hat and parade up and down his street!

2. Put an ad in your local paper saying how much you fancy him and asking if he'd like to go out on a date!

3. Bake him a cake and decorate the top with sugar love hearts and deliver it to his door!

4. Get a job baby-sitting his little sister five nights a week!

5. Ask him to come round and help you fix your bike!

6. Bribe your chemistry teacher into inventing a love potion and put it in his Pepsi!

7. Make your big brother become his best mate. That way he'll be round at your house lots!

8. Pop round to his house and ask if you can borrow his heavy metal records!

9. Offer to carry his books to school — every day!

10. Whenever he and his band are playing, go along and cheer enthusiastically — even if they're awful and are playing in his dad's garage!

11. Write his name all over your school books and casually drop them at his feet!

get him to you!

Is that boy of your dreams ignoring you? Do you ever feel as if he doesn't know you exist? Well, try our top 25 tips to get yourself noticed and knock him out!

12. Send him a Valentine — even if it's November!

13. Become a cheerleader for the school football team and only chant his name!

14. If you're going to a Christmas party and you know he'll be there, stand close to him at all times so that one of your friends can keep popping up and putting mistletoe over your heads!

15. Throw a huge party at your house when your parents are on holiday and make him the guest of honour!

16. Go round to his house and tell him that you're selling kisses for charity and insist he buys at least ten!

17. Drop your purse outside his gate! He'll have to bring it back and you can ask him in so that you can thank him properly!

18. Write a love song for him and enter the Eurovision Song Contest with it!

19. If you don't get that far, simply serenade him under his bedroom window!

20. Ask him to dance the Military Two Step with you at your school Christmas party and whizz him off his feet to the nearest piece of mistletoe!

21. Train your pet terrier to run up and grab his leg whenever it sees him!

22. Frantically splash past him at the local swimming pool — he'll always remember you as the girl who nearly drowned him! You could always offer him the kiss of life!

23. If it's really busy on the school bus, get up and offer him your seat!

24. "Accidentally" skate into him at the roller disco and offer to rub his sore bits!

25. And finally — give him your last Rolo!! Aaaw!

KEEPIN' COSY'S NEVER LOOKED SO GOOD! GRAB A PAIR OF WALKING SHOES AND HEAD FOR THE COUNTRY IN CORDED FASHION . . . !

Country

Cords...

SWING COAT; from **SNOB**
FLORAL SHIRT; from **C & A**
SKI PANTS; from **TOP SHOP**
AIR FORCE BOOTS; from **THE EMPIRE CATALOGUE**

HOODED JACKET; from **SNOB**
CORDUROY JODHPURS; from **HENNES**
FLORAL BLOUSE; from **BHS**
SOCKS; from **THE SOCK SHOP**
SHOES; from **CURTESS**

DENIM JACKET; from **C & A**
CORDUROY WAISTCOAT; from **FLIP**
CORDUROY JODHPURS; BY **KUMAR** from **TOP SHOP & C & A**
SHIRT; from **BHS**
BOOTS; from **THE EMPIRE CATALOGUE**

ARAN JUMPER; from **C & A**
CORDUROY SKIRT; from **HENNES**
SHOES; from **DOLCIS**
TIGHTS; from **THE SOCK SHOP**
BRACELET; from **TOP SHOP**

CORDUROY JACKET; from **HENNES**
MOTIF JEANS; from **TOP SHOP**
AZTEC CORDUROY SHIRT; from **HENNES**
LEATHER SATCHEL; from **RIO**
SHOES; from **DOLCIS**

DENIM JACKET; from **THE KIT CATALOGUE**
CORDUROY SKI PANTS; from **BHS**
POLO NECK JUMPER; from **THE EMPIRE CATALOGUE**
SHOES; from **CURTESS**

THE LIFE OF KYLIE!

. . . is a many splendoured thing, so we raided the "Kyles files" to find out the best-kept secrets of our favourite songstress!

- Her star sign is Gemini.
- She drinks thyme tea.
- Just call her "crinkly-clothes" 'cos she hates hanging up her "garments"!
- She liked playing Charlene 'cos she was a real bossy boots.
- She's a birrova shoe freak.
- Her hero is Prince.
- When she was a teeny little girl she wore wellies with smileys on the toes!
- Her first crush was on a huge hunk in Grade 3.
- She's got her own house in Melbourne and she spends yonks decorating it.
- She cooks a mean banana pie.
- Her favourite food is chocolate and she indulges in chocolate sarnies!
- The first book she read twice was 'The Lion, The Witch And The Wardrobe'.
- She's "rubbish" at deciding what to wear and she usually ends up trying on about 10 different "outfits".
- She's a real perfectionist!
- Her heroines are Audrey Hepburn and Katherine Hepburn 'cos she loves 50's actresses.
- Madame Tussauds has a waxwork dummy of her.
- She's got relatives in Wales!
- She first met Jason when she was 11 and remembers him as "really chubby with a bowl haircut". (Cheek!)
- She and Jason went on hols to Bali to get a rest from the "hurly-burly", but it *was* just as friends!!
- Her most annoying habit as far as Jason is concerned is that she picks her lips!
- Her favourite silly "news"paper story was . . . "Is Kylie Minogue An Alien?"

Melanie was about to find out that even she couldn't handle this pizza the action — even if he was a Jason Donovan lookalike.

MAKING my way back to the table, I couldn't help smirking a bit.

"Melanie Fisher, you jammy devil!" Lorna said through gritted teeth. "How did you do it? How did you get talking to him?"

"Just my natural charm," I said, taking my seat and turning round to give a final wave to Gary, the Jason Donovan lookalike behind the counter.

Suzanne and Lorna both groaned.

"Three weeks we've been coming in here and got nowhere," Suzanne moaned. "Then the first time we bring HER . . ."

"Yeah, I know." Lorna sighed. "All that money I wasted on bodyspray as well. That advert's a con."

"Oh, and talking of money . . ." I interrupted. "There was the small matter of a bet. Fifty pence each, I believe."

"That was only if you got him to ask you out somewhere," Lorna said smugly.

I gave them a cocky smile. "Like to the pictures tonight, you mean?"

Suzanne and Lorna looked at each other, then, groaning again, they both reached into their pockets and slammed the coins down on the table.

"Thank you," I said with a smile.

We sat in silence for a few minutes before Lorna spoke again.

"OK," she said. "So now we've paid up you could at least tell us what you did."

They looked at me expectantly. I took a deep breath, opened my mouth to speak, and the waitress arrived.

"Right," she said. "Two cheese and tomato?"

"Here," Lorna and Suzanne said as if in stereo.

"So . . ." the waitress went on, looking at me with a grin, ". . . you must be the pepperoni and chocolate spread."

When she'd gone we all stared at the thing nestling on my plate. Brown squidgy sauce with bits of pink pepperoni poking up here and there.

"Mel, you idiot," Suzanne said, "you'll make yourself ill."

"Yeah, you will." Lorna nodded. "Yeuck!"

I looked at the pizza, then at them. "Don't be stupid," I said. "You don't

IZZA THE ACTION!

think I'm really going to eat it, do you? I'll just take it out under my jacket and bin it in the street."

"It made him notice me."

Lorna poked it with her knife as if to see if it was alive.

"It's still a waste of money," she said.

"Is it?" I gave a broad smile and turned to give Gary a wave. "It made him notice me, didn't it?"

Suzanne sighed. "Why didn't we think of that?"

"Well you didn't, did you?" I snorted, cutting the pizza up into quarters for easy disposal. "So just pass me a few serviettes and shut your . . ."

"Hello," a cheery male voice said.

"Oh . . . er . . . hi," I said, looking up at him. "Er . . . Gary, these are my mates, Lorna and Suzanne."

"Hi." He gave them a beaming smile, then turned back to me. "How's the pizza?"

"Fine," I said, gulping a bit. "I'm . . . er . . . just waiting for it to cool down. Don't want to burn my mouth."

"Course you don't," Gary said. He glanced round the table again. "That's some mate you've got," he said to the others.

"We know," Lorna said, sneering.

Gary put his hand on my shoulder, smiled right in my eyes, and then laughed. "Pepperoni and chocolate spread." He grinned. "That is really the weirdest topping I've ever had to do."

"I was just thinking, Mel." Suzanne looked at me deliberately. "That pizza must be cool enough to eat now."

"Yeah," Lorna said with a wide smile. "Mine is." She picked up a corner and munched it. "Come on," she said. "Tuck in."

I looked daggers at them both, then up at Gary.

"Er . . . shouldn't you be getting back to work?"

He glanced round over his shoulder. "No," he said. "It's my break. I've got ten minutes yet."

"Right," I said. "Here goes."

As I took the first bite I closed my eyes, but it didn't help. It was disgusting. I needed all my courage to swallow.

"Is it all right?" Suzanne said, giggling into her serviette.

"Oh . . . lovely," I said, trying to smile but unable to force the corners of my mouth up. "Mmm! Delicious!"

BY the time I'd got half-way through, Gary's break was over.

"Well," he said, getting to his feet. "I'll see you tonight, then. Half seven, OK? Enjoy your meal."

When he'd gone, Suzanne and Lorna just about fell apart laughing.

"Delicious!" Lorna

spluttered.

"Lovely!" Suzanne laughed, the tears streaming from her eyes.

"Yeah," I said, getting up and bunging the last of it into a wad of serviettes. "Go on, you can laugh. I'll be the one laughing tonight, though, when I'm snuggled in the back row with Gary and you two are stuck at home watching Les Dawson!"

And I stormed off home, hopping mad.

It was about an hour later that it started. I was watching T.V., drying my hair, and planning the evening ahead. First I thought it was just nerves.

"Melanie? Are you all right?"

I glanced up at Mum, who was ironing in front of the telly.

"Yeah, I'm fine," I said. "Just thinking about Gary."

Mum smiled over Dad's shirt-sleeves. "I don't know," she tutted. "You and your boyfriends'll be the death of me. You really . . . Melanie? What's the matter?"

"Nothing," I said, holding my stomach. "I'm . . . er . . . just going to the loo."

It was half an hour later I came out looking decidedly pale. "Melanie!" Mum fussed. "What's the matter? You look awful, you're as white as a sheet."

I walked slowly over to the mirror. She was right.

"I can tell you right now," Mum said, "I don't care how good-looking this Gary is, there's no way you're going out tonight."

I opened my mouth to argue, then shut it again. It was time to go back to the loo.

"Don't mention bananas."

At half past six I knew. No way was I going to make it to the pictures to meet Gary. Miserably, I picked up the phone and dialled Lorna's number.

"What do you mean, go instead of you?" She sounded as if she couldn't believe her ears. "Have you gone bananas or what?"

"Don't mentior bananas."

"What?"

"Don't mention any food, in fact," I said in a puny voice. "I've spent the last three hours throwing up."

"Hey," Lorna said. "You know what — I reckon it was that pizza."

"Oh, how very clever of you," I said sarcastically. "Now shut up about it, right, or I'll ask Suzanne instead."

"All right," Lorna said, still sniggering. "What do I tell him then?"

I sighed. "Just say I've got a cold."

The night was long. Half past seven came and went. I lay on the sofa wrapped up in a blanket and imagined Lorna snuggling up to Gary.

"All right, love?" Mum looked at me. "Shall we have Les Dawson on?"

"Yeah," I said grimly. "Why not."

DING dong! The doorbell startled us both.

"Ooh, I wonder who that can be?" Mum said, looking at her watch. She went out to the hall. I heard voices, and then she came in again, smiling.

"You've got a visitor," she said.

I saw him like a vision, coming through the door. It couldn't be, but it was. Gary. Dressed up really nice, clutching a carrier bag in his hands.

"Gary," I said, "what are you doing here? Why aren't you out at the pictures?"

"With your mate?" he came and sat down next to me on the sofa. "That wouldn't be very nice, would it, with you at home ill?"

I took a deep breath in and sighed with happiness. Out of the corner of my eye I could see Mum looking on approvingly. He was getting Brownie points all round.

"So," he said, "how are you feeling now, then? Is your cold any better?"

Mum cleared her throat in the background. She was trying not to laugh.

"Er . . . excuse me," she said. "I've just remembered I've got something in the oven."

"It was that pizza."

When she'd gone, I looked at Gary, feeling about one inch high. "I've . . . er . . . got a confession," I said. "It's not a cold. It was that pizza. I . . . er . . . don't think pepperoni and chocolate spread really agrees with me."

"But I thought you said . . .?"

"Yes, I know." I looked at the carpet, ashamed. "I . . . sort of lied. Well, not sort of. Just lied. I wanted to get you to notice me, so I made up something really outrageous."

"You didn't need to." He grinned. "I noticed you the moment you came in."

"Did you?"

"Mmm."

I looked at him and smiled.

"Oh well," I said, twirling the corner of the blanket between my fingers. "Never mind. Everything has turned out OK now, hasn't it?"

"Not quite."

"Why?"

Gary reached into his bag and brought something out. A present. He didn't open it, but he didn't need to. It was a plastic take-away tray, still greasy, still warm, with chocolate sauce beginning to seep from out the sides.

"What on earth do I do with this?"

THE END

JACKIE
JASON
SHOT: LFI

BODY TALK

GROWING UP'S NOT ALWAYS EASY, ESPECIALLY WHERE YOUR BODY'S CONCERNED. THERE ARE ALL SORTS OF CHANGES HAPPENING, SOME OF WHICH CAN BE PRETTY SCARY IF YOU DON'T KNOW WHAT'S GOING ON. SO READ ON, AND PREPARE YOURSELF WITH OUR HANDY GUIDE.

HORMONES

Putting it as simply as possible, hormones are responsible for the changes going on in your body. They tell your body that the time has come to move on from being a girl to a woman. As well as the obvious signs, starting periods and developing a bust, there are lots of other things that can happen too. One of the most frightening things about the changes you're going through is the way you may feel. One minute you're on top of the world, and the next you'll be crying your eyes out! It's not easy getting your emotions under control when hormones are playing havoc with your system. The important thing to remember, though, is that this is perfectly normal and that you will learn how to cope with these new feelings.

PERIODS

Periods are, of course, the biggest change your body is going to go through. Every girl is an individual and when you start your periods can vary greatly, so don't worry if all your friends have started and you haven't yet — it's just a matter of time. Roughly speaking, though, you should get your first period between the ages of nine and 17. How do you know when your first period is going to start? Well, if your breasts have begun to develop, your pubic hair has started to appear and you have a slight discharge from your vagina, then your periods should be along fairly soon. It's a good idea to carry a sanitary towel or tampon with you if you think your periods may start soon. Don't worry yourself sick that it will start suddenly and embarrass you, all that'll happen is that you'll probably notice a few red or brownish spots of blood when you go to the toilet.

The average period lasts for 4-6 days and the average menstrual cycle is 28 days, but this is just an average and yours may well differ from this.

BREASTS

Like periods, breasts vary greatly from person to person. No-one can tell whether you'll take a 36C cup by the time you're 14, or a 32AA at 17. Try not to worry about it too much — the size of your bust has absolutely nothing to do with anything.

Your breasts don't always develop at the same rate, either. It may make you feel rather self-conscious that one of your breasts is larger than the other one, but remember that you have plenty of time for the other breast to catch up.

STRETCH MARKS

As well as developing breasts you'll also probably find that you put on weight around your bottom, hips and thighs. This is all part of developing "womanly curves" and is perfectly natural. However, you may find that your skin has not kept pace with the growth and you end up with stretch marks. These are purplish-red coloured threads under the skin and are caused by your skin's elasticity being stretched to its limit — as happens when you grow suddenly. Take heart, though, stretch marks do eventually fade.

SPOTS

When you've got spots you feel as if everyone is staring at you. However, since over 70% of teenagers suffer from spots, your friends are more likely to be worrying about their *own* skin rather than yours! If you do have spots, there are several ways you can help yourself:

- Don't pick! You may spread the infection and you also increase the chances of the spot leaving a scar.
- Keep your hair and hands away from your face, as both tend to be a bit greasy.
- Keep your skin clean. If you find soap too drying, use a medicated cleansing bar.
- Try out the various spot treatments available from chemists.

● If your spots are really bad ask your doctor if he/she can prescribe something to help.

BODY HAIR

Like everything else, the amount of body hair you have varies from person to person and if you're naturally dark-haired it may seem a bit more noticeable. Absolutely everyone has body hair, so it's nothing to be embarrassed about or ashamed of, but if you'd prefer to get rid of the hair on your legs or underarms there are several ways you can do it:
Shaving: Either wet using an ordinary razor (very cheap!) or dry using an electric shaver. Both are quick and easy, but hair regrows after about three days.
Depilatory creams: This is a bit more messy and time consuming than shaving, but you should stay hair-free for almost a week.
Waxing: There are cold wax strips you can use at home or you can go to a beauty salon and have it done professionally which is a bit more expensive. Both are rather painful!
Bleaching: This is probably the best treatment for facial hair, but make sure you use a bleach specially made for your face. Facial hair should never, ever be shaved off.

PERSONAL HYGIENE

Make sure that you take particular care over your personal hygiene at this time. You will start to perspire more and this can have a very unpleasant smell if you don't wash frequently and use a deodorant of some sort. Here are a few things you can do to make sure you're nice to sit next to!
● Have a bath or shower every day to keep you smelling fresh and clean.
● Have an all-over wash with soap and water if a bath or shower is not possible. It's just as effective.
● Always pay particular attention to underarms, between your legs and your feet as these are the places where the sweat glands are most active.

HELP!

If you're worried about any health matter or think something strange is happening to your body, don't bottle up your fears. Nine times out of ten your mum or other female relative will be able to put your mind at rest. If you do need to see the doctor, there's no need to get all worked up or embarrassed about it. The doctor will have heard your problem many times before and won't think you're silly or pass judgement. If you'd rather see a female doctor, ask at the reception as this is usually easily arranged.

FOLLOW OUR GUIDE TO LOOKING GROOVY AND SKIN AND HAIR PROBLEMS WILL BECOME A THING OF THE PAST!

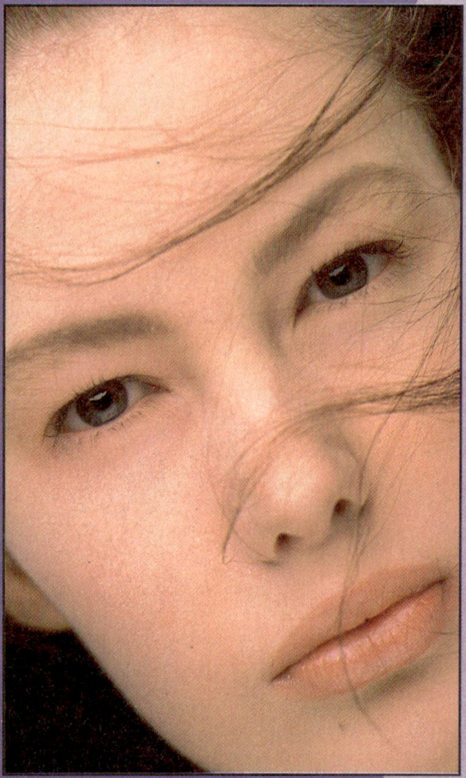

SKIN

● First, the basics. Make sure you cleanse, tone and moisturise twice a day, whatever your skin type. It's definitely worth it!

● If your skin's on the oily side, don't abandon moisturiser altogether because it helps your skin to retain water and keep it soft. Go for a light, oil-free make such as Pure & Simple.

● Prone to ruddy cheeks? Invest in some green-tinted moisturiser or powder. Worn under make-up it's a positive miracle worker.

● Once a week use a deep-cleansing face mask. Choose one for your skin type and remember to follow the instructions to the letter!

● A facial scrub will rid you of dead, dull skin and brighten your complexion no end! Don't 'scrub' though — choose a gentle one and just massage it gently over your skin.

● If you're prone to zits and other nasties, avoid facial scrubs — they can spread infection and make your skin a million times worse!

● Positively the worst thing you can do to your skin is go to bed leaving all your make-up on — yeuch! It's a killer and, what's more, in the morning your eyes will be glued shut by half a ton of gunk! No matter how tired you are, always take off the slap before bed!

● If you're rushed in the morning and don't have time to apply a full face, go for some tinted moisturiser, a coat or two of mascara and some lippy — it shouldn't take more than five minutes to apply the lot.

● Trying to rid yourself of spots is a dodgy business! Opt for a product containing benzoyl peroxide. Stick with it for a while — it won't work overnight. If there's no improvement after a couple of months, visit your doctor.

● Finally, sleep. There's no point in lavishing care and attention on your skin if you don't get enough kip. We're not saying don't be a rock and roll child, but try to get a reasonable sleep of a night. A good trick, if you've been having many a wild night, is to catch up on some shut-eye at weekends!

HAIR

● When washing your hair don't make the water too hot, as this will only stimulate the oil glands in your scalp and make your hair greasy. Rinse with icy cold water to give your locks a glossy shine.

● Healthy hair starts on the inside, so eat lots of nutritious scoff, and concentrate on getting lots of wheatgerm and vitamin B rich foods — go for lots of green veg and wholemeal bread in particular.

● Going for a regular trim won't make your hair grow faster (that's just an old wives'

lookin

tale!) but it will keep it in good condition. Every couple of months should be sufficient.

● If your hair is subjected to many an "appliance" such as hairdryers, straighteners, hot bendy sticks etc., give it a once a week deep-conditioning treatment to keep it soft and well-conditioned.

● Naturally curly or permed hair? Invest in a diffuser for your dryer — it'll dry your hair without making it frizzy.

● If you're a sporty girl and enjoy regular swims — beware! Chlorine can be especially drying to your hair, so always condition well after a dip.

● If you want to put your hair up or try a new styling "technique", don't wash it immediately beforehand. Wash it the day before and it will be much easier to deal with.

● Nowadays, most people use quite a lot of gel, mousse, hairspray etc. While this isn't in itself harmful, it can cause 'build-up' on your hair, making it dull and lifeless. To combat this use a special shampoo designed to get rid of build up — try Neutrogena's fabby shampoo.

● Avoid back-combing. It's well dodgy for your hair.

● There's no harm in washing your hair daily if you feel that's what it needs, but make sure that you use a gentle shampoo. You shouldn't need to lather more than once!

Shot courtesy of Vidal Sassoon

’ good!

All I want for

All Lisa wanted for Christmas was . . . a solution to her problem!

Christmas . . .

AND . . .
SO WHAT IS IT YOU WANT TO TALK TO ME ABOUT? IS IT THE REASON YOU'VE BEEN SO QUIET THIS WEEK?
YOU NOTICED THAT? I THOUGHT I WAS GETTING AWAY WITH IT!
I'VE KNOWN YOU A LONG TIME, LISA. C'MON, TELL YOUR OLD FRIEND HERE WHAT'S WRONG.
IT'S PETE AND WHAT TO GET HIM FOR CHRISTMAS. I REALLY LIKE HIM, KATE, BUT I JUST DON'T KNOW WHAT TO DO ABOUT HIS PRESENT.
YOU HAVEN'T BEEN GOING OUT VERY LONG, HAVE YOU?
SEVEN WEEKS. IS IT TOO SOON TO EVEN GET HIM A PRESENT? WHAT IF I DO AND HE DOESN'T?
"IT WOULD BE JUST AWFUL IF . . ."
PETE! YOU SHOULDN'T HAVE! I MEAN, I DIDN'T . . .
I JUST HOPE YOU LIKE IT, LOVE. I CAN EXCHANGE IT IF YOU DON'T.
LIKE IT? I WOULD DIE OF EMBARRASSMENT RIGHT THERE ON THE SPOT!
WHY DON'T YOU GET HIM SOMETHING SMALL, THEN? YOU KNOW, A SORT OF TOKEN GIFT?
LISA'D THOUGHT OF THAT, TOO . . .
I REALLY LIKE THE SOCKS YOU GOT ME, LISA — THEY'RE JUST WHAT I NEED. DO YOU LIKE THE SOLID GOLD LOCKET AND CHAIN I GOT YOU?
OH, PETE, I DON'T KNOW WHAT TO SAY . . . YOU SHOULDN'T HAVE SPENT THIS MUCH!
IT'S HOPELESS, ISN'T IT? I'D BE AS WELL FALLING OUT WITH HIM BEFOREHAND AND FORGETTING THE WHOLE THING!
OH, LISA, YOU'RE A NUTCASE, DO YOU KNOW THAT? WHY DON'T YOU JUST GET HIM A RECORD TOKEN AND LET HIM CHOOSE HIS OWN GIFT?

A RECORD TOKEN? THAT WOULDN'T SHOW MUCH THOUGHT, WOULD IT?
LISA, SANTA DOESN'T PUT THIS MUCH THOUGHT INTO CHRISTMAS PRESENTS! STOP TORTURING YOURSELF OVER THIS, WILL YOU?
IT'S OK FOR YOU! YOU'VE BEEN GOING OUT WITH BRUCE FOR AGES. YOU EVEN KNOW WHAT SIZE JEANS HE TAKES, FOR GOODNESS' SAKE!
ONLY BECAUSE I ASKED HIM, YOU IDIOT! WHY DON'T YOU TRY IT? TALK TO PETE. WHO KNOWS? HE MIGHT BE GOING THROUGH THIS AGONY OF INDECISION TOO!
DO YOU THINK SO? I DON'T KNOW, KATE. MAYBE HE WASN'T PLANNING ON GETTING ME ANYTHING ANYWAY. WOULDN'T THAT BE AWFUL . . .? HEY, WHERE ARE YOU GOING?
AWAY FROM YOU BEFORE I DO SOMETHING DRASTIC! GIVE ME A RING LATER ON IF PETE AND YOU FANCY JOINING BRUCE AND I AT THE DISCO TONIGHT. I'VE HEARD ENOUGH ABOUT CHRISTMAS PRESENTS FOR ONE DAY!
YOU'RE NOT LEAVING ME TO SORT THIS OUT ON MY OWN, ARE YOU? A MINUTE AGO YOU SAID YOU WERE ONE OF MY OLDEST FRIENDS!
YEAH, I AM. SO HOW COULD I HAVE FORGOTTEN WHAT YOU'RE LIKE? YOU'RE THE ONLY PERSON I KNOW WHO COULD MAKE CHOOSING BETWEEN TWO EYE SHADOWS SEEM A LIFE OR DEATH DECISION! SEE YOU LATER, LISA!
HUH! IT'S ALL RIGHT FOR KATE. SHE AND BRUCE ARE PRACTICALLY ENGAGED! I COULDN'T ASK PETE WHAT SIZE JEANS HE WORE. I CERTAINLY COULDN'T AFFORD A PAIR FOR HIM, EITHER!
AND . . .
I COULD AFFORD THAT SILVER TIE-CLIP IF I GOT DAD TO GIVE AN ADVANCE ON NEXT WEEK'S POCKET MONEY . . . THE TROUBLE IS I'VE NEVER SEEN PETE WEARING A TIE. I DON'T KNOW IF HE EVEN OWNS ONE!

SPEAK OF THE DEVIL . . .
HI, THERE — I THOUGHT IT WAS YOU, LISA. CHRISTMAS SHOPPING?
YES, I AM. HELLO, PETE.
WHAT WERE YOU LOOKING AT IN THERE?
OH, ER . . . CUFF-LINKS FOR MY DAD. YOU KNOW WHAT FINDING A PRESENT FOR DADS IS LIKE!
SALE SALE
25%
I HAVE THAT PROBLEM WITH EVERY PRESENT! DO YOU KNOW I'VE BEEN LOOKING ALL DAY AND I'VE BOUGHT ABSOLUTELY NOTHING YET?
I CAN BELIEVE IT. I'VE HAD EXACTLY THE SAME TROUBLE!
WHAT DO YOU SAY WE JOIN FORCES FOR THE LAST HOUR, THEN? YOU KNOW WHAT THEY SAY ABOUT TWO HEADS BEING BETTER THAN ONE.
WHY NOT? I'M WILLING TO TRY JUST ABOUT ANYTHING!
IT WAS THE MOST FUN LISA HAD HAD ALL DAY . . .
WHAT ABOUT THIS FOR MY LITTLE BROTHER, SAM? DO YOU THINK HE'D LIKE IT?
IT'S MILES TOO BIG FOR SAM! IT WOULDN'T EVEN FIT YOUR DAD.
YEAH, YOU'RE RIGHT, I SUPPOSE. SO MUCH FOR MY MUM'S THEORY ABOUT GROWING INTO THINGS!
AND . . .
MY MUM LIKES THAT PERFUME, BUT I'D NEED FOURTEEN PAPER ROUNDS BEFORE I COULD AFFORD TO BUY IT FOR HER! SOMETIMES I THINK IT'S KIND OF CRAZY, ALL THIS RUSHING ROUND SPENDING MONEY ON CHRISTMAS PRESENTS.
YEAH, I KNOW WHAT YOU MEAN . . .
AND THEN I MEET SOMEONE I LIKE AND SUDDENLY IT DOESN'T SEEM SO CRAZY ANYMORE. I'D REALLY LIKE TO BUY YOU A CHRISTMAS PRESENT, LISA.
YOU WOULD?
THE ONLY PROBLEM IS YOU'RE GOING TO HAVE TO CHOOSE SOMETHING YOURSELF. I'M AFRAID I'M HOPELESS AT PICKING PRESENTS, AND I JUST DON'T WANT TO MAKE A MISTAKE WITH ONE AS IMPORTANT AS YOURS.
OK, THEN. I'LL AGREE ON ONE CONDITION . . .
AND WHAT'S THAT?
THAT YOU DO THE SAME. I CAN'T THINK OF A SINGLE SOLITARY THING TO GET YOU, PETE. IN FACT, YOUR PRESENT'S BEEN SPOILING THE THOUGHT OF CHRISTMAS FOR ME!
SPOIL CHRISTMAS? WE CAN'T HAVE THAT! DON'T YOU KNOW THAT CHRISTMAS IS REALLY SPECIAL? IT'S THE ONLY TIME OF YEAR THAT MISTLETOE COMES OUT, FOR ONE THING!
AND WE CAN'T LET THAT GO TO WASTE, CAN WE? MERRY CHRISTMAS, PETE — YOU'RE PRETTY SPECIAL YOURSELF . . .
SO ARE YOU, LISA. AND I'LL TELL YOU SOMETHING ELSE — CHRISTMAS THIS YEAR IS GOING TO BE PERFECT, JUST YOU WAIT AND SEE!
THE END

chatting up is hard to do!

OK, OK, I suppose you lot think boys have jolly, old lives, eh? Running around, "getting off" with at least half a dozen girlies a night, and then swaggering off to boast about their exploits to a gang of mates? Well, let me just inform you, if you know anyone who acts like that, then they're not a boy — they're an entirely different species altogether; Latin name: cretinus cretinus. Most of us boys are shy, tender, sensitive types. What do you mean you don't believe me? Huh, thanks a lot!

Unfortunately, it's just these lads who seem to have got one thing down to a very fine art — chatting-up. Don't ask me how they do it (except do, please!) because apart from your mum forcing you to wear those ghastly mustard loon-pants she bought triumphantly at the Women's Guild sale-of-work for you, there is nothing more cringe-worthy than trying to chat up some female you fancy like rotten.

DON'T TALK RUBBISH!

"Don't talk rubbish!" I hear you yell. "You just have to come up and talk to us, that's all." Oh yeah, is that right? There certainly aren't many of your sort left, are there? Nope, the way I see things is more like this . . .

You lot sit there, looking thoroughly bored out of your pretty li'l skulls, while we — the poor, sweating, gibbering, "stronger" sex — attempt to break the ice with a whole host of delightful one-liners and clichés. Except that's impossible, because the ice tends to be thicker than Antarctica! It's true, believe me! You don't help much, do you? It's all very well and fine to bat those eyelashes at us, but as soon as we're over — zoooooom! — the barriers come slamming down! Blimey, it's enough to make a grown 17-year-old cry! (Boo hoo hoo!)

Our pals don't help much either, though. They'll yank you into the toilet at break and tell you, in hushed tones, if you really want to

go out wih Amanda McKinley (the school vamp — 5′ 7″; long, red hair; moves in 14 opposite directions when she walks!), all you have to do is hit her with the right chat-line and, bingo!!! She'll be proverbial putty in your mitts! Oh joy of joys, you may think, but why is it these so-called surefire "pulling" lines always fall flat on their faces, either leaving you with a mighty slap mark across your gob, or the sound of hysterical laughter ringing in your ears for months to come? Here're a few examples, for instance:

CHAT-UP LINES

1) "Hey, funky baby-cakes. Your transmitter's tuned into my wavelength and I'm picking up your hot vibes loud and clear on my lurve transmitter." Hmmm, this one only works in 1970's American movies where all the girls have horrific middle-partings and seven inches of make-up, and you wouldn't touch them for all the dosh in the world!

2) "I'm really sorry to barge in like this but I really do like you." Oh, nooooo!! You might have been a wimp before, but what do you honestly expect girls to think of you after this "gem"?

3) "Giz a snog, doll!" Yes, well, a little too far in the other direction! As long as you're good at ducking, you might escape a black eye or two!

4) "Excuse me, but would you like a bit of my kebab? There's some very tasty olives in there, you know!" Now, I tried this one myself once and it didn't go down too well at all. How was I to know her ex-fiance worked in Kaleb's Krazy Kebab Kabin?

Chatting-up's a funny old game, isn't it? One boy tells his story about the ups 'n' downs of trying to impress the gals!

They're just a few of the more colourful attempts, as the "Don't I know your face?/Don't tell me, you're a model, aren't you?/Here I am — the hunk of your dreams!" school of thought is definitely a bit dated these days!

WHAT CAN A POOR BOY DO?

So what can a poor boy do? Just give up and retreat back to his bedroom, and listen to all his dreary Smiths records again and again? Dream hopelessly about whisking your "lady" from the nearest Wimpy and taking her away from it all? Yup, that's what I do, anyway! At 17, I'm a veteran of this chat-up lark and it's got me absolutely nowhere. In fact, I'm giving up girls altogether and going back to marbles and train-spotting. Nah, I've had enough to last me a lifetime — a last-ditch effort to impress Julie Sachs ("You know, hon, me and you could really go places — savvy?") has just confirmed it further!

Anyway, who needs girls? I don't, do I? 'Course not! Even that new girl who's just moved in two doors away — nah, ain't worth the bother, is it? She is really nice-looking, though — but I wouldn't stand a chance, would I? Hold on, there is that new line my mate, Jim, told me — something like "Please tell me your name because last night in my dreams I could only call you baby"! Says it will work wonders, he does. Well, I suppose I could have one more go; nothing ventured, nothing gained! But if it doesn't work this time, I'm definitely giving up for life! Well, maybe . . .

"Don't I Know You

We bounded heartily out on to the streets to find out what you girls (and a few select boys!) think of this chatting-up business . . .

Neil

Right, mate! What's the worst chat-up line you've ever used?

"Well, erm, I once said to a girl, 'I'm famous!! Who are you?!' I've been trying to live it down ever since!"

Fabsy, we're sure. Who would you most like to chat up?

"Molly Ringwald — yum! But I'd hate to be chatted up by Kylie, though."

Do you think it's up to boys to do all the chatting-up?

"No, that's not right. Girls should try to meet us halfway, I think."

Sharon and Wendy

What's the worst chat-up line you've been confronted with?

Sharon: "'You look like somebody I know' and 'Do you come here often?' — they've both been tried on me."

Wendy: "Guys are always saying I look like Steffi Graf. Weird, eh?"

Do you think boys are any good at chatting-up?

Sharon: "It depends. I'd rather boys just acted themselves, really."

Wendy: "Ha ha, most of them are useless! At least you get a laugh, though!"

Ashley and Lisa

Well, girls! What's the tackiest line anybody's ever hit you with?

Ashley: "Oh, someone once said to me, 'I know you from somewhere, don't I?' That was really embarrassing, especially as I'd never seen him before in my life!"

Lisa: "Yeah, that one's been tried on me before. Ugh!"

Do you think it should be left to boys to do all the chatting-up?

Ashley: "No, I think it should be equal."

Lisa: "I'd agree with that. It's only fair, isn't it?"

Who would you love to be chatted-up by?

Ashley: "Hmmm! Matt Dillon — he's gorgeous!"

Lisa: "River Phoenix, definitely River Phoenix!"

From Somewhere?"

Rhona

OK, girlie, what's the worst chat-up line you've ever heard?

Rhona: **"My fiancé grabbed me at school and yelled, 'You're working with me in Biology, right!'"**

Oo-er, and you got engaged to this bloke!?!

Anyway, d'you think boys should do all the chatting-up?

"No, I don't think girls really try at all. It puts all the pressure on the boys."

Jennifer and Carol

Do you think it should be up to the poor boys to do all the chatting-up?

Jennifer: **"Yeah, I think they should. If they're interested in a girl, then they should do something about it, shouldn't they?"**

Carol: **"No, I think both people should make a bit of effort."**

Who would you hate to be chatted-up by?

Jennifer: **"Pat Sharpe! He's really 'orrible-looking, isn't he?"**

Carol: **"I'd hate to be chatted-up by Jason Donovan."**

Jane and Joan

Guff chat-up lines, girls?

Jane: **"A really disgusting boy once told me I was the girl of his dreams! Honest, he did!"**

Joan: **"Would you believe me if I told you someone once said to me, 'I've seen you somewhere before, haven't I?'"**

Who'd you most like to be chatted-up by?

Jane: **"Kevin Costner or Marti Pellow."**

Joan: **"Tom Cruise but definitely not Bros!"**

Lisa and Susan

What's the most awful chat-up line you've ever "encountered"?

Lisa: **"A guy once said to me, 'Do you come here often?' I can't believe that — it's so smarmy, isn't it? Yuk!"**

Susan: **"If anybody ever came up to me and said 'You're a model, aren't you?', I think I'd crack up laughing!"**

Who'd you like to wander up to you and chat you up?

Lisa: **"Tom Cruise — he's dead gorgeous, isn't he?"**

Susan: **"Mel Gibson, he's a hunk."**

Do you think it's flattering to be chatted-up?

Lisa: **"Of course! Does the world of good for the old ego!"**

Susan: **"As long as they're nice-looking, ha ha!"**

David and Craig

What's the worst chat-up lines you've ever heard?

David: **"'What are you doing tonight?' That's just the worst."**

Craig: **"Erm, I dunno. I wouldn't use corny lines like that!"**

Who would you just lurve to chat-up?

David: **"Kelly McGillis, if I got the chance!"**

Craig: **"Yeah, I fancy her, too. I'd hate to chat-up Margaret Thatcher!"**

leg it!...

For Pretty Pins — Walk This Way!

Designed opaque tights; by Mary Quant from Mary Quant
Skirts by CCC from Top Shop
Pumps; from FHW

Lacy and panel tights; both from Top Shop
Skirts by CCC (as before)
Pumps; from FHW

Glitter tights (available in gold and silver); from Top Shop
Skirt by CCC (as before)
Shoes; from Saxone

Bright opaque tights; by Aristoc from leading department stores
Blue knitted skirt; by Jeffrey Rogers from Top Shop
Pink pumps; from Miss Selfridge
Purple lycra skirt; by CCC from Top Shop
Purple pumps; from Dolcis

From hand-painted to Aztec; from Top Shop

Gold embroidered socks; from The Sock Shop

Ankle socks; from a selection at Tokyo Boogie Beat, 17 Shorts Gardens, London, WC2 (phone 01-379 4338 for mail order details).

Wacky designs; from Miss Selfridge

Ankle socks; by Burlington at major department stores

Designer patterned knee-hi's; from The Sock Shop

Lynx 'STOP' socks; from The Lynx Shop, 79 Long Acre, Covent Garden, London, WC2 (phone: 0371 872016 for mail order details)

Argyll socks; and cuff socks; from a selection at Woolworth
Suede pumps; from Miss Selfridge

Classic knee-hi's; by Burlington from major department stores
Suede Chukkas; from Shelleys

Bow 'n' Bell socks; from C&A
Crêpe sole pumps; from Saxone

Patterned thigh-hi's; from The Sock Shop

Animal socks; from a selection at Woolworth

Wacky designs; by Extras at Dolcis

Photographer: Mike Davis

JACKIE
NEW KIDS ON THE BLOCK
SHOT: JULIAN BARTON

NIGHTMARE ON ELLIE'S STREET

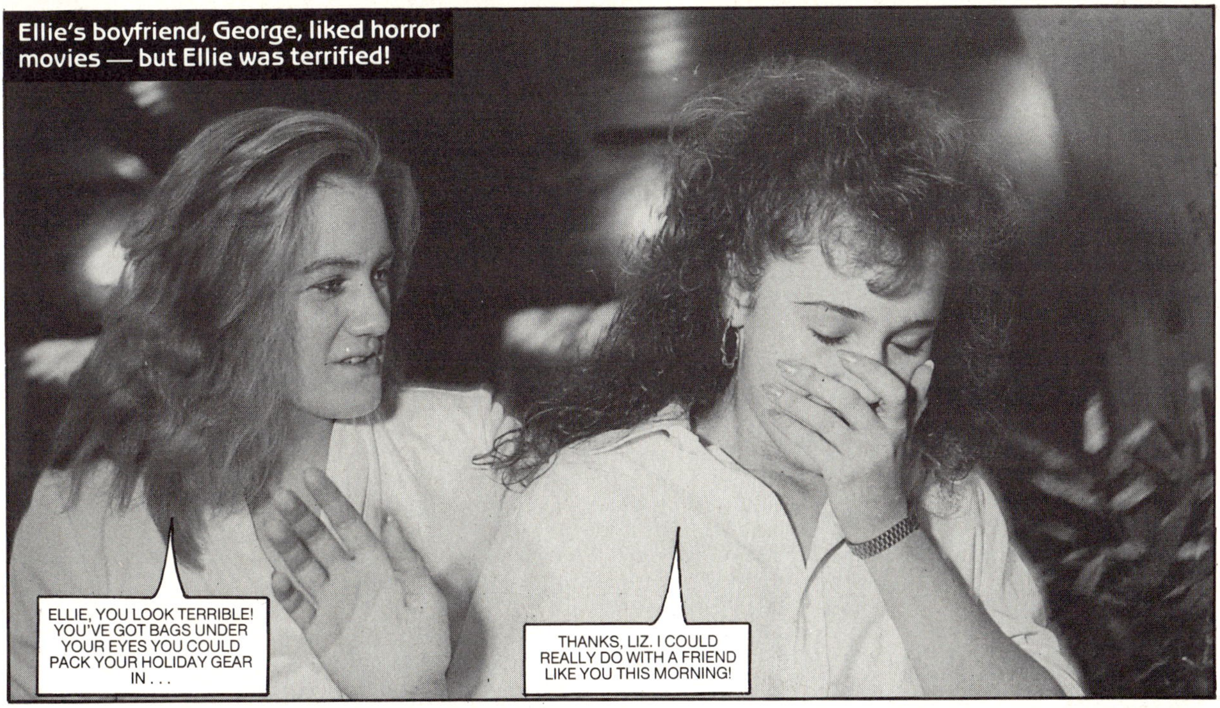

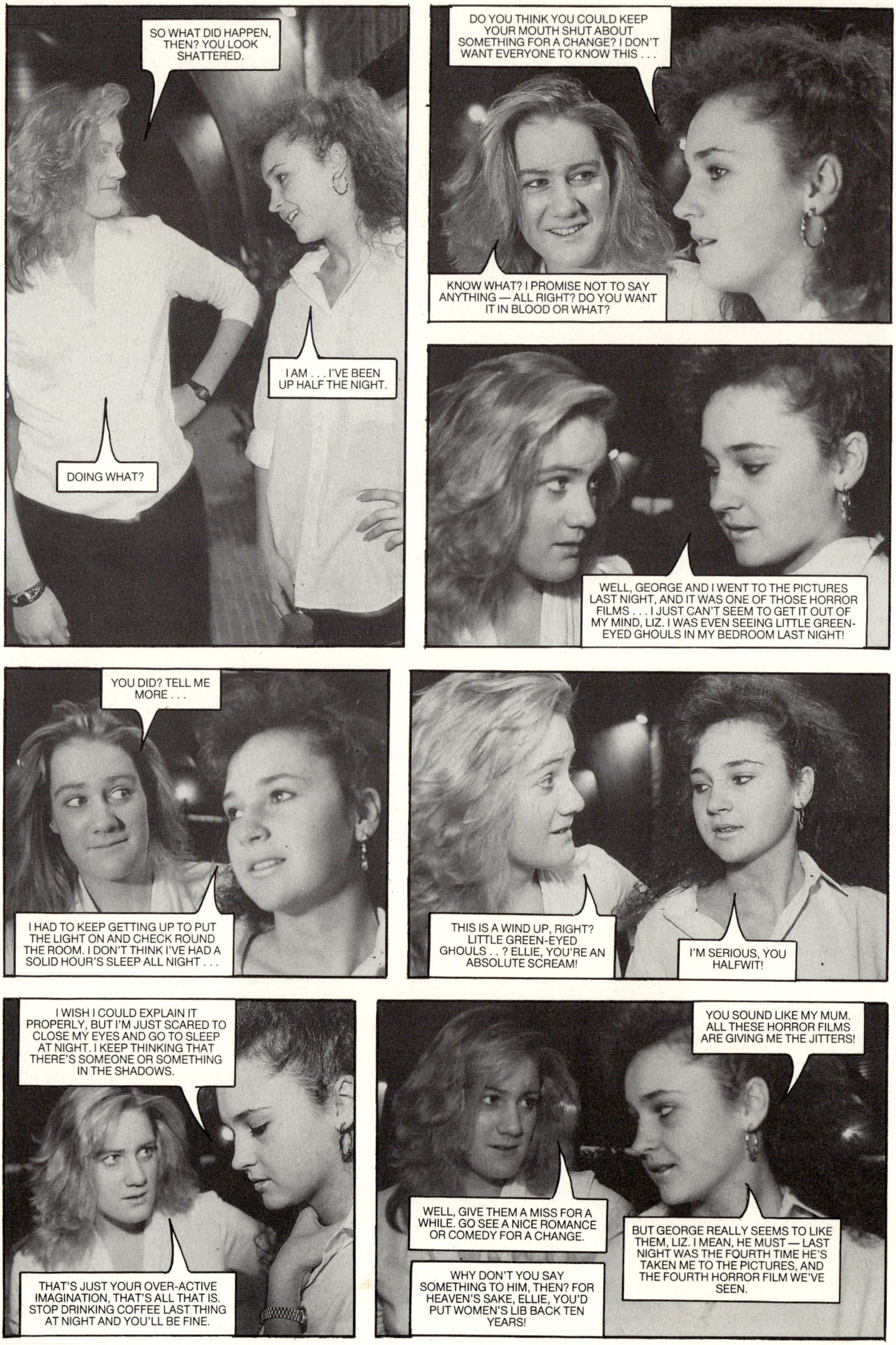
SO WHAT DID HAPPEN, THEN? YOU LOOK SHATTERED.
I AM . . . I'VE BEEN UP HALF THE NIGHT.
DOING WHAT?
DO YOU THINK YOU COULD KEEP YOUR MOUTH SHUT ABOUT SOMETHING FOR A CHANGE? I DON'T WANT EVERYONE TO KNOW THIS . . .
KNOW WHAT? I PROMISE NOT TO SAY ANYTHING — ALL RIGHT? DO YOU WANT IT IN BLOOD OR WHAT?
WELL, GEORGE AND I WENT TO THE PICTURES LAST NIGHT, AND IT WAS ONE OF THOSE HORROR FILMS . . . I JUST CAN'T SEEM TO GET IT OUT OF MY MIND, LIZ. I WAS EVEN SEEING LITTLE GREEN-EYED GHOULS IN MY BEDROOM LAST NIGHT!
YOU DID? TELL ME MORE . . .
I HAD TO KEEP GETTING UP TO PUT THE LIGHT ON AND CHECK ROUND THE ROOM. I DON'T THINK I'VE HAD A SOLID HOUR'S SLEEP ALL NIGHT . . .
THIS IS A WIND UP, RIGHT? LITTLE GREEN-EYED GHOULS . . ? ELLIE, YOU'RE AN ABSOLUTE SCREAM!
I'M SERIOUS, YOU HALFWIT!
I WISH I COULD EXPLAIN IT PROPERLY, BUT I'M JUST SCARED TO CLOSE MY EYES AND GO TO SLEEP AT NIGHT. I KEEP THINKING THAT THERE'S SOMEONE OR SOMETHING IN THE SHADOWS.
THAT'S JUST YOUR OVER-ACTIVE IMAGINATION, THAT'S ALL THAT IS. STOP DRINKING COFFEE LAST THING AT NIGHT AND YOU'LL BE FINE.
YOU SOUND LIKE MY MUM. ALL THESE HORROR FILMS ARE GIVING ME THE JITTERS!
WELL, GIVE THEM A MISS FOR A WHILE. GO SEE A NICE ROMANCE OR COMEDY FOR A CHANGE.
BUT GEORGE REALLY SEEMS TO LIKE THEM, LIZ. I MEAN, HE MUST — LAST NIGHT WAS THE FOURTH TIME HE'S TAKEN ME TO THE PICTURES, AND THE FOURTH HORROR FILM WE'VE SEEN.
WHY DON'T YOU SAY SOMETHING TO HIM, THEN? FOR HEAVEN'S SAKE, ELLIE, YOU'D PUT WOMEN'S LIB BACK TEN YEARS!

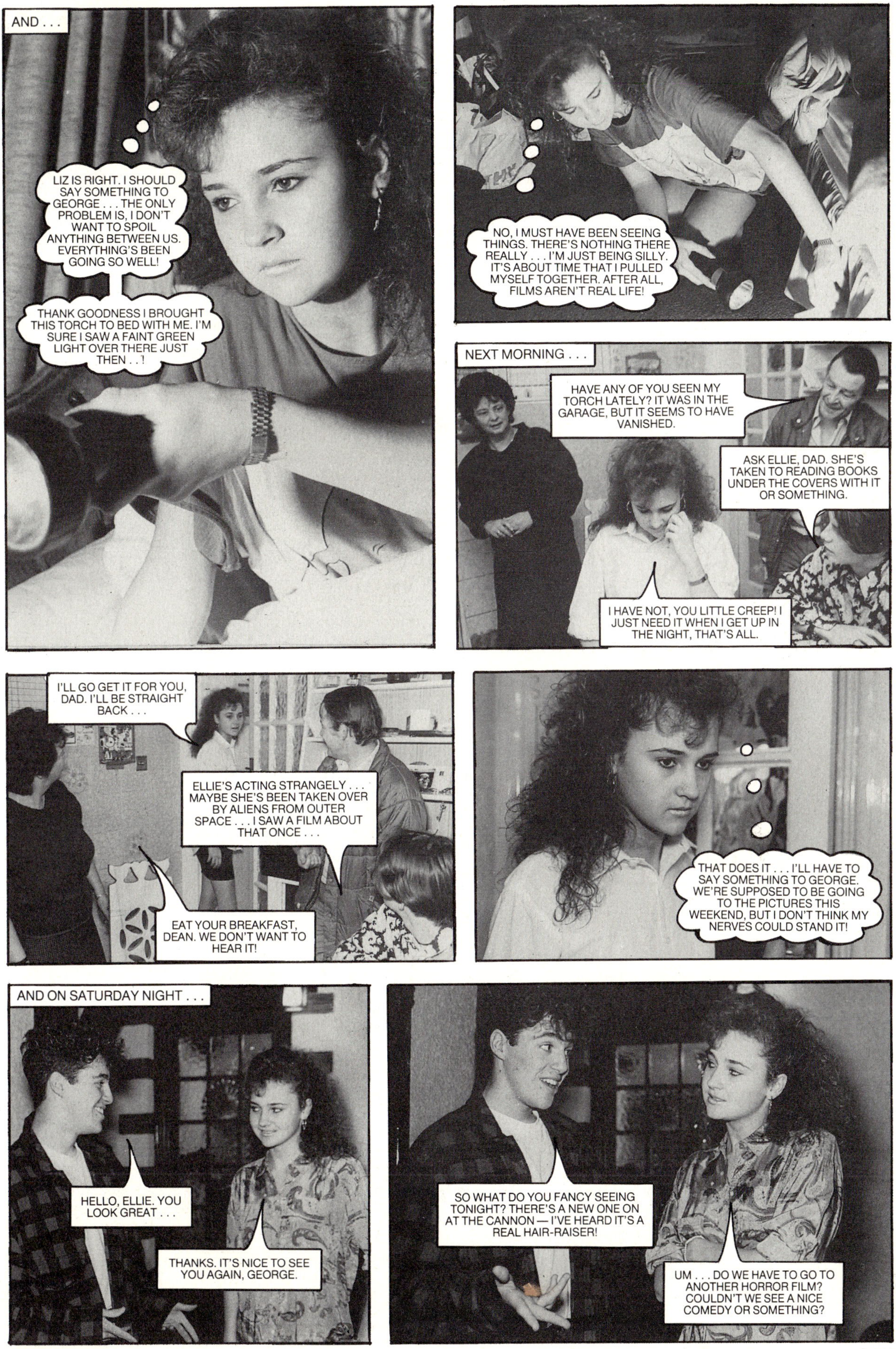
AND . . .
LIZ IS RIGHT. I SHOULD SAY SOMETHING TO GEORGE . . . THE ONLY PROBLEM IS, I DON'T WANT TO SPOIL ANYTHING BETWEEN US. EVERYTHING'S BEEN GOING SO WELL!
THANK GOODNESS I BROUGHT THIS TORCH TO BED WITH ME. I'M SURE I SAW A FAINT GREEN LIGHT OVER THERE JUST THEN . . !
NO, I MUST HAVE BEEN SEEING THINGS. THERE'S NOTHING THERE REALLY . . . I'M JUST BEING SILLY. IT'S ABOUT TIME THAT I PULLED MYSELF TOGETHER. AFTER ALL, FILMS AREN'T REAL LIFE!
NEXT MORNING . . .
HAVE ANY OF YOU SEEN MY TORCH LATELY? IT WAS IN THE GARAGE, BUT IT SEEMS TO HAVE VANISHED.
ASK ELLIE, DAD. SHE'S TAKEN TO READING BOOKS UNDER THE COVERS WITH IT OR SOMETHING.
I HAVE NOT, YOU LITTLE CREEP! I JUST NEED IT WHEN I GET UP IN THE NIGHT, THAT'S ALL.
I'LL GO GET IT FOR YOU, DAD. I'LL BE STRAIGHT BACK . . .
ELLIE'S ACTING STRANGELY . . . MAYBE SHE'S BEEN TAKEN OVER BY ALIENS FROM OUTER SPACE . . . I SAW A FILM ABOUT THAT ONCE . . .
EAT YOUR BREAKFAST, DEAN. WE DON'T WANT TO HEAR IT!
THAT DOES IT . . . I'LL HAVE TO SAY SOMETHING TO GEORGE. WE'RE SUPPOSED TO BE GOING TO THE PICTURES THIS WEEKEND, BUT I DON'T THINK MY NERVES COULD STAND IT!
AND ON SATURDAY NIGHT . . .
HELLO, ELLIE. YOU LOOK GREAT . . .
THANKS. IT'S NICE TO SEE YOU AGAIN, GEORGE.
SO WHAT DO YOU FANCY SEEING TONIGHT? THERE'S A NEW ONE ON AT THE CANNON — I'VE HEARD IT'S A REAL HAIR-RAISER!
UM . . . DO WE HAVE TO GO TO ANOTHER HORROR FILM? COULDN'T WE SEE A NICE COMEDY OR SOMETHING?

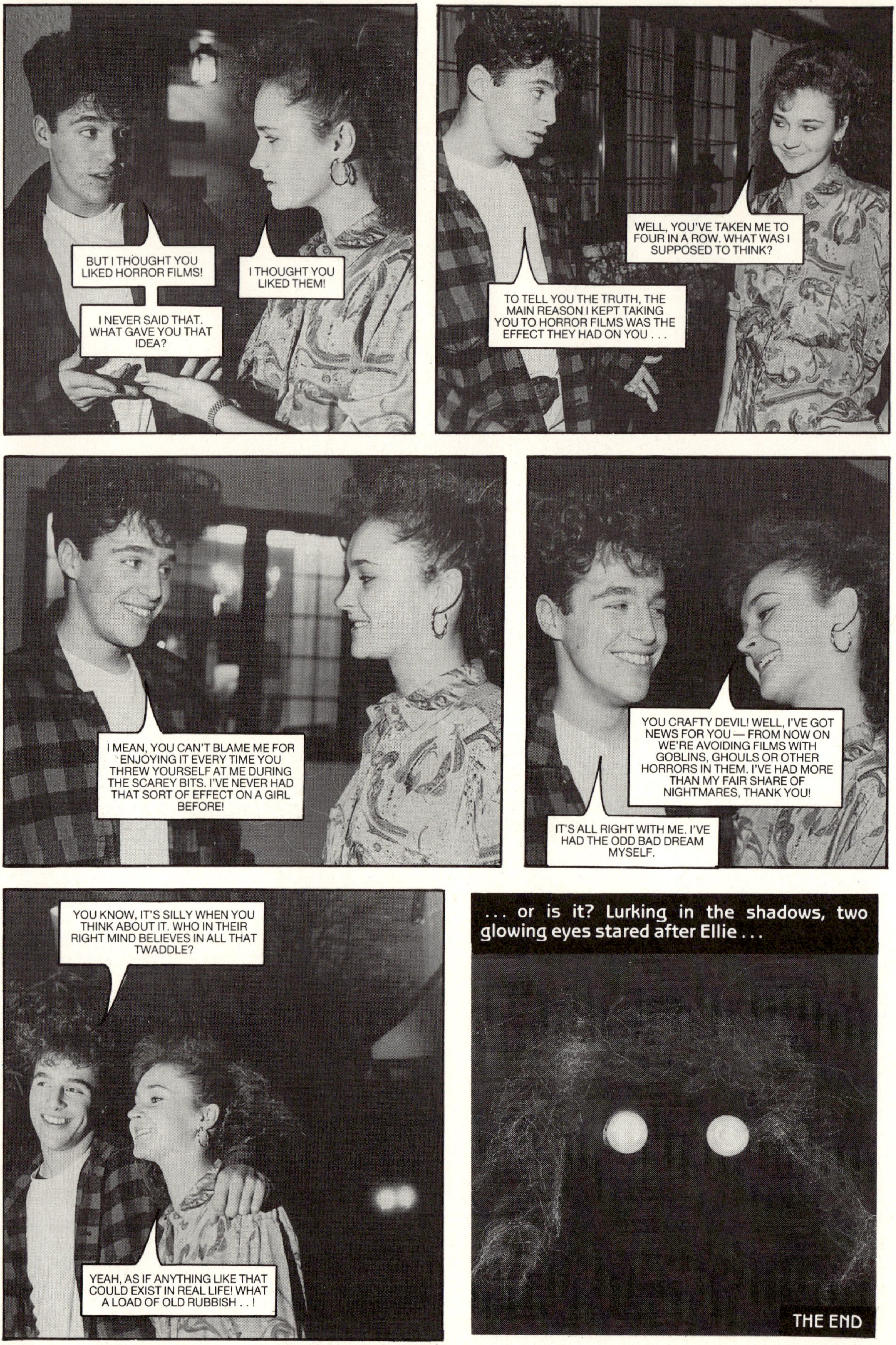
BUT I THOUGHT YOU LIKED HORROR FILMS!
I THOUGHT YOU LIKED THEM!
I NEVER SAID THAT. WHAT GAVE YOU THAT IDEA?
WELL, YOU'VE TAKEN ME TO FOUR IN A ROW. WHAT WAS I SUPPOSED TO THINK?
TO TELL YOU THE TRUTH, THE MAIN REASON I KEPT TAKING YOU TO HORROR FILMS WAS THE EFFECT THEY HAD ON YOU . . .
I MEAN, YOU CAN'T BLAME ME FOR ENJOYING IT EVERY TIME YOU THREW YOURSELF AT ME DURING THE SCAREY BITS. I'VE NEVER HAD THAT SORT OF EFFECT ON A GIRL BEFORE!
YOU CRAFTY DEVIL! WELL, I'VE GOT NEWS FOR YOU — FROM NOW ON WE'RE AVOIDING FILMS WITH GOBLINS, GHOULS OR OTHER HORRORS IN THEM. I'VE HAD MORE THAN MY FAIR SHARE OF NIGHTMARES, THANK YOU!
IT'S ALL RIGHT WITH ME. I'VE HAD THE ODD BAD DREAM MYSELF.
YOU KNOW, IT'S SILLY WHEN YOU THINK ABOUT IT. WHO IN THEIR RIGHT MIND BELIEVES IN ALL THAT TWADDLE?
YEAH, AS IF ANYTHING LIKE THAT COULD EXIST IN REAL LIFE! WHAT A LOAD OF OLD RUBBISH . . !
. . . or is it? Lurking in the shadows, two glowing eyes stared after Ellie . . .
THE END

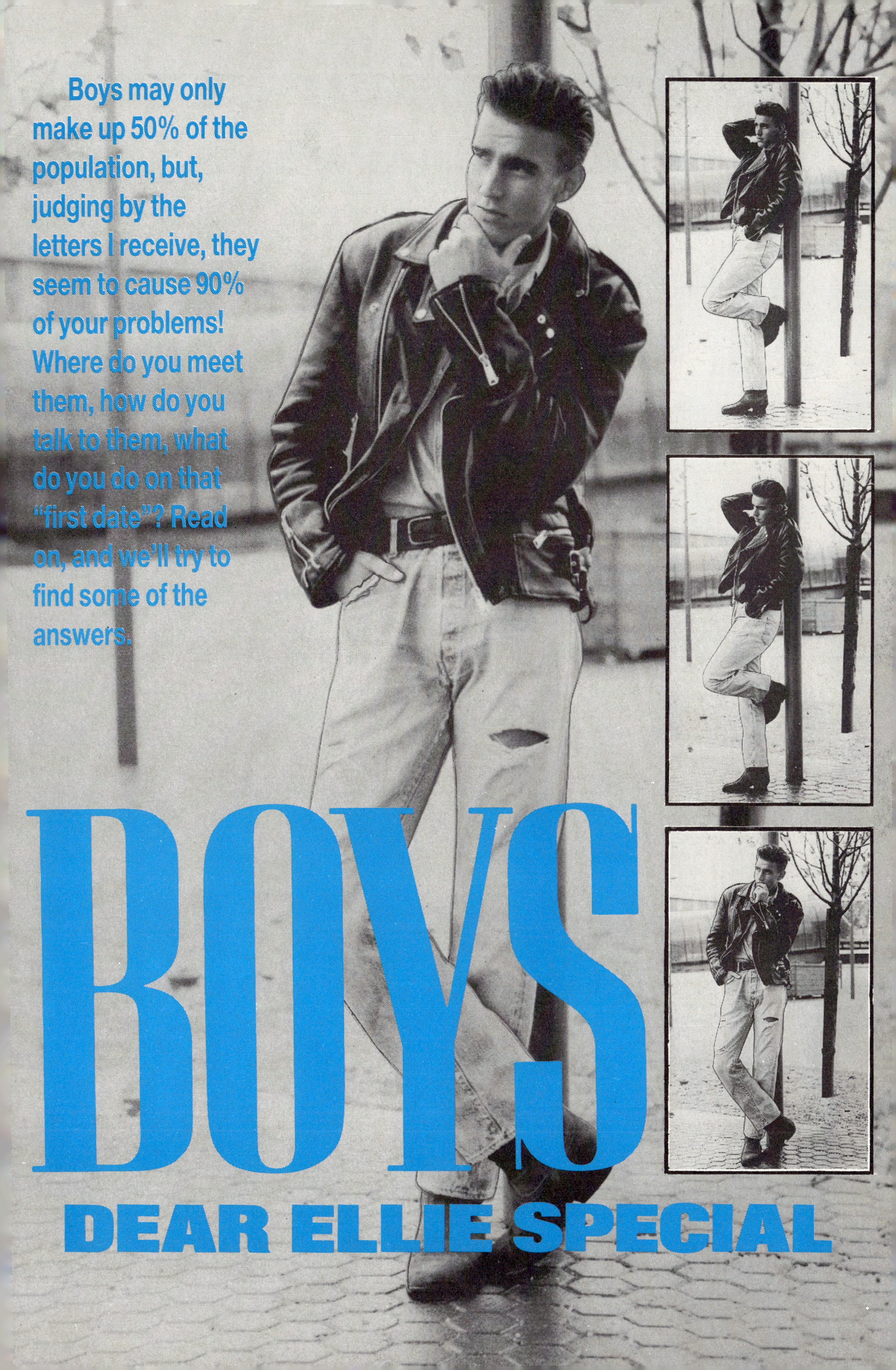

Boys may only make up 50% of the population, but, judging by the letters I receive, they seem to cause 90% of your problems! Where do you meet them, how do you talk to them, what do you do on that "first date"? Read on, and we'll try to find some of the answers.

BOYS

DEAR ELLIE SPECIAL

WHERE TO

● **SCHOOL:** Unless you're at an all-girls' school, this is the best place to start getting to know boys — OK, so Tom Cruise might not be working in your geography class, but where else would you get the chance to meet so many boys the same age as yourself? The big advantage of meeting boys at school is that it shouldn't be impossible to find something you have in common that you can talk about, whether it's just shared subjects and teachers, mutual friends or the school canteen! And you'll always be able to find someone who knows the boy you've got your eye on, so you can work out whether he's got a girlfriend, what his interests are, etc.

● **DISCOS/PARTIES:** These can be great for meeting boys, simply because one of the main reasons people go to them is to eye each other up and have fun. However, it can sometimes be tricky trying to chat up someone you don't know. The

HOW TO TALK TO THEM

Really this shouldn't be any more difficult than talking to your mates or anyone else, but of course it often is! If you fancy someone, or think they might fancy you (especially if you don't know them very well) it can seem almost impossible to find the courage to start chatting to them. But if you *don't*, how will he ever know what you're like, or guess that you may be interested in him? Remember:

● Boys are only human! He'll probably be flattered you've made an effort to approach him, same as you would be if things were the other way round.

● Be yourself. Don't try to put on an act to impress him — it won't work!

● It doesn't have to be amazingly witty. Often just smiling at someone and saying hello is enough to break the ice.

● If you're shy — and lots of people are — it won't necessarily work against you. As long as you say *something* (so he knows you're not stuck-up, boring or not interested in him) shyness can be quite appealing. It's usually a lot more attractive than someone who's absolutely full of themselves and doesn't stop talking.

MEET THEM

other disadvantage is that you'll tend to be attracted to someone mostly on the strength of their appearance, which is often no guarantee they're nice underneath, or compatible with you.

● **THROUGH FRIENDS:** Every girl knows some boys, even if they're brothers, the lad next door, an ex-boyfriend or a distant cousin. OK, none of them may be YOUR ideal man, but they may be the perfect match for a friend, so introduce them around!

● **CHANCE MEETINGS:** Lots of girls seem to nurse secret hopes that they'll meet the Boy Of Their Dreams by accident one day while out walking the dog, buying a magazine at the corner shop or waiting for a bus, and that he'll take one look at you and fall madly in love. Well, OK, it happens in stories and *sometimes* in real life — but not that often, so don't stare at every half-decent boy who passes by as if this could be *him!*

WHY DOESN'T HE FANCY ME?

Practically every girl knows what it feels like to spot a boy you fancy, plot elaborate schemes to get talking to him, only to get precisely nowhere — he just doesn't seem to notice you.

We receive dozens of problem letters about this, and the writer of every letter thinks it must be because there's something wrong with *her*, because otherwise what can she be doing wrong?

Unfortunately, our answer nearly always has to be the same — you can't *make* someone fancy you. Just think for a moment of all the boys you know who you wouldn't really want to go out with, for one reason or another. Not because they're ugly, boring or stupid, but maybe because you simply don't *feel* anything for them. No-one really knows why we fancy some people and not others — it's just that certain "something" that attracts you to someone, but if it's not there you can't do anything about it.

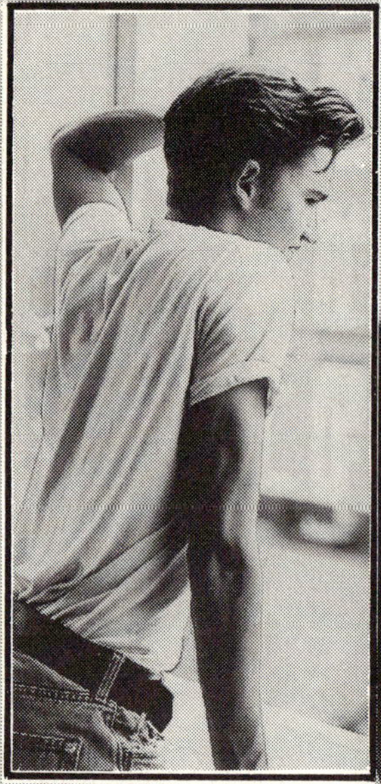

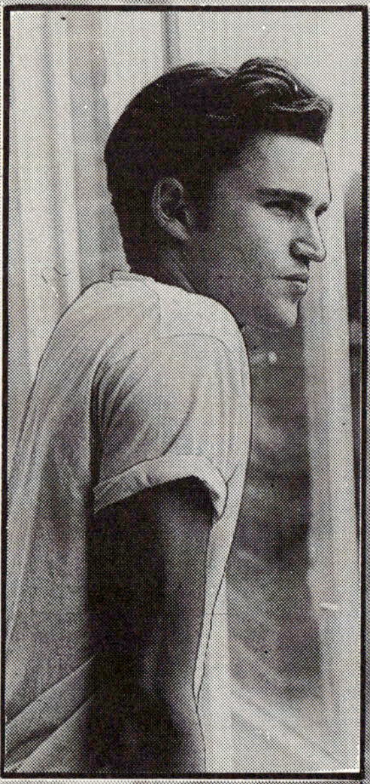

ASKING

Obviously there can't be any hard-and-fast rules here — a lot will depend on your individual situation, and how well you know each other. But there are a few important things to remember which might help:

- Never get friends to do the "dirty work" for you. Lots of girls chicken out by getting their mates to tell his mates you like him, or pass on notes to him, or arrange meetings on your behalf. The big danger with this, though, is that he may suspect you or his mates are just having a joke at his expense. You're going to have to face him sooner or later, so pluck up your courage and do it now!
- If you are serious about this, try to arrange at least some dates out of

THEIR

Girls often imagine they're the only sensitive ones — the only ones who get nervous and shy, the only ones to get mad crushes on people, or hurt in relationships, or who worry about their appearance and whether anyone will ever fancy them. Well, boys can, and do, feel exactly the same way — they're just more used to hiding it, or covering it up by pretending not to care. Boys generally don't talk to each other about their fears and feelings in the way that girls do, which is a pity, because it often means they

GOING OUT WITH THEM

- Don't expect it to be the romance of the century and get deadly serious about it. Relationships are supposed to be fun, and you're asking to be disappointed if you expect too much too soon or imagine he'll be some sort of romantic hero.
- A lot of girls who write to us think a boyfriend is some sort of miraculous cure for everything that's wrong in their lives — they think he'll be a constant provider of kisses, cuddles and affection. Well, he might be if you're very lucky, but he'll also introduce a whole new lot of worries and cause as many problems as he solves!
- Don't drop your friends in his favour — you'll probably want them long after he's been forgotten!

HIM OUT

school. You can't conduct a proper relationship while all your mates are gawping at you.

● Don't be too disappointed if he seems to like you but won't actually ask you out. He may not want a proper relationship just yet — boys mature more slowly than girls. Or he may not be allowed to, for that matter — it's not just girls who have strict parents, you know!

● If you ask him out and he says no, it's not the end of the world. You may feel embarrassed about it, but you always take that risk when you ask someone out. That's why it's a good idea to really find out how keen a boy is before you jump in with both feet.

FEELINGS

end up all desperately trying to impress each other instead of being honest with themselves.

It isn't just boys who hurt people and let their partners down — girls can be thoughtless, spiteful and nasty too, and boys take things to heart the same way you do! Never mess a boy around or deliberately play games with him just because you think he can handle it or will know it's a joke — he may be more affected by it than you imagine.

BOYS AND SEX

A lot of girls worry about how they'll cope if and when a boy asks them to have sex with him. Many are afraid that if they say no they'll lose their boyfriend, or be labelled "frigid" or "childish" if they say they're not ready or not sure.

We've said it before, but it's always worth repeating; sex should be kept for a secure, loving, trusting relationship, and of course, until you're mature enough to make that decision — the law says that until you're 16 you shouldn't have to face that problem. If you're under 16, or simply feel you're not ready for a commitment like that, it's your right to say no. Never agree to sex as a way of keeping someone or of curing any other problems in your relationship — if he cares so little about you he'll pressure you into doing something you're not ready for, he's unlikely to stay with you for long whether you sleep with him or not.

Your boyfriend may love you but if that's the case, he won't be the type to drop you or turn nasty just because you don't feel ready.

BREAKING UP

Relationships can often be pretty short-lived, especially when you're young, and can break up as quickly as they started. Lots of boys, sadly, don't seem to be able to end a relationship properly. They'll often take the coward's way out — suddenly ignoring you, sending a message through someone else, or just standing you up. It's partly because they're not always too good at explaining their feelings — perhaps they're not even sure what those feelings are exactly. Sometimes it's because they don't want to "get serious" — they may feel they're missing out on something, or their mates are encouraging them to "play the field". That can be very hard for you to accept, especially if you felt things had been going well between you; it's always easier if you have a proper explanation to hang on to. If this happens to you and you do still want to go out with him, the best you can do is make it clear that if he changes his mind you'll still be interested — then try to get over it in your own time.

Bear all this in mind, though, if you're finishing with him. Never be nasty about it or try to get revenge by spilling all his secrets and faults to your mates and his. If it gets around you're the type who spreads tales at the end of a relationship you may find new boyfriends few and far between.

A CLEAN BREAK

A soppy story by Carol Marsh

"YOU wanted to see me?" Jayne tried to sound formal.

But as Steve stood up, her heart hammered, and she nearly dropped the note she noticed she was still stupidly clinging to. The note he'd put through her letterbox before she was even up this morning.

"Yes. I hope you don't mind coming here." He indicated the wide green expanse of the park. "But I thought we could walk, and it'd be more . . ."

"Neutral?" Jayne turned from him, jamming her hands into her pockets, crushing the note. As he fell into step beside her, she tried not to remember all the times they had spent here over the past year. Holding hands. Laughing. Sheltering in the bandstand. Kissing.

It had all been so special. And now, thanks to one stupid quarrel, it was all over.

"Did — did you get your books and tapes?" As she spoke, he turned to look down at her. And she had to catch her breath. She realised she had forgotten how being close to him had always made her feel.

"Yes, thanks." He sighed, and looked quickly away, his face pale and his eyes in shadow, "but you needn't have posted them, Jayne. I — I was going to come round . . ."

"Oh?" Crazy hope lit up inside her, and went out again just as quickly as she remembered the heat of the quarrel. The way they had never, in the whole year they'd been together, shouted at one another like that. And all over something trivial — she could barely remember how it even started.

"Yeah." He glanced quickly at her, seeing the conflict in her set face at the painful memory. "I — I wanted to make sure I hadn't left anything behind . . ."

Instinctively, they had stopped walking, standing side by side, looking across towards the children's playground. A toddler, wrapped warmly against the evening air, was climbing the steps of the slide, encouraged by his anxious parents.

"How's Ben?"

Steve watched the scene in silence for a while, and then cleared his throat. "How's Ben?" he asked, awkwardly.

Jayne felt her insides contract. She'd been waiting for this but it didn't make it easier. Stepping away from him she continued walking, he followed.

"F-fine," she said, over brightly. "Same as ever, a little bigger . . ."

"I — I've missed him," Steve admitted. He stopped again, sinking on to a bench. As she sat beside him, Jayne found herself remembering.

Steve and her in her room at home, close and happy and loving. Even her parents had liked him, and she swallowed, recalling the worried look on her mother's face when she knew they had parted.

"Ben's three months old now," she heard herself say, remembering the special day like it was yesterday. "It doesn't seem possible."

"I KNOW." He looked down at her again, his dark eyes suddenly full of memories, too. His mouth smiling in the way she thought she had forgotten. "Everybody said we were really stupid . . ."

"Wondering how we'd cope!" She smiled too, thinking of those moments when the two of them had seemed so united, and because of that, against all the odds, so strong.

"Maybe we were stupid," she finished, deflatedly, shivering at the thought. "After all, look at us now!"

He nodded and sighed, and suddenly there didn't

seem anything else to say. Jayne got to her feet. "I think I'd better go," she said, looking at her watch. "Mum's keeping an eye on him but it's not really fair . . ."

"Wait a minute!" Steve got to his feet and stood facing her, blocking her path. "I haven't said all I came to say, yet. About Ben . . ."

"But . . . ?" Jayne's throat was suddenly tight. For the first time ever, she felt as if he were some sort of opponent. It was an uncomfortable feeling. "Look, just don't think you're taking him!" she exclaimed, holding out her hands as if to ward off a physical attack. "Ben's mine! And don't you forget that!"

Steve reached out and took her hands. His touch was, surprisingly, as gentle as it was firm. "Ben's *ours*, Jayne!" he corrected, quietly. "We agreed that from the beginning — remember?"

As his eyes met hers, Jayne slowly nodded. Another memory filled her, of Steve stating, between kisses, what he considered to be his rights.

She could hardly breathe.

"We might not be married — yet," he'd said, that day they became a happy threesome, "but he's as much mine as yours. He's — well — part of our future as well as all we've shared already. OK?"

"What do you want to do?" she asked, now. He was staring at her, and she could hardly breathe.

In answer, he drew her closer, and she felt the warmth and comfort of his arms like a haven. "I want fair access of course," he said quietly, relaxing. "And I reckon that means seeing Ben most nights of the week!"

"Just . . . ?" Jayne's heart gave a great jump, and she could hardly speak for happiness. "Just like you did before, you mean?" she whispered, and looking up at him, seeing the shadows lifting from his eyes. "That does mean seeing *me* too, you know — not just Ben . . . ?"

"So? Who's complaining?" Gently, Steve bent his head and kissed her, and it was as if the park were suddenly full of fireworks. The quarrel, and its painful consequences had completely vanished.

"Let's go home," she suggested, slipping her hand into his. "There's a very impatient puppy waiting for us!"

THE BEST PART OF BREAKIN' UP IS WHEN YOU'RE MAKIN' UP!

— Or so they say! We take a good ol' look at both sides and see which gives you the biggest reason to blub!

Breakin' Up...

Aaah, no-one said this was easy — no matter who does the chucking! But sometimes being a free gal again can be a barrel o' laughs! So if you've recently "parted company" with your boyfriend, don't weep buckets, get a look at this — and smile!!!!

THINGS YOU CAN'T DO IF YOU'RE GOING STEADY!

Remember — it's fun to be free!

1. Have totally outrageous nights on the town with all your mates, boy-hunting!
2. Flirt shamelessly with every male specimen that comes your way!
3. You can't lie in bed all day on a Sunday, because you would have to go round and have tea with his granny!
4. You can't dance insanely at the disco withou worrying if you'll embarrass your "click"!
5. Lounge around the house in your tatty old pyjamas and your dad's socks, in case he pops round unexpectedly!

HOW TO BREAK UP AND NOT MUCK UP

Yus, how to chuck someone without too much hassle!

. Flirt with every boy you see and really heese him off!
. Refuse to take any of his phone calls and lon't answer the door when he comes round!
. Get one of your mates to tell him for you! An easy one this!)
. Tell him you're madly and passionately in ove with someone else! (Even if you're not!)
. Tell him to his face that he's chucked! (This s the quickest and simplest way!)

THE BEST BITS ABOUT BREAKIN' UP!

You might not believe it, but breaking p can be a bit of a giggle!!! Here's why . . .

. You can scream and shout and be very dramatic!
. It'll give you a chance to return (ie. throw back) all ose naff little pressies he gave you!!!
. If he's done something mean to you, you can embarrass him by chucking him in front of his mates! (Nasty, but fun!)
4. You can use long, long boffin-like words and totally confuse him!
5. Think how good he'll look wearing that chocolate milk shake that you're about to pour over him!!!

HOW TO GET OVER BREAKIN' UP!

If you find yourself moping around the house, then cheer yourself up by trying out a few of this lot!!!

1. Go crazy with your barnet and dye it a very risque blonde colour!
2. Phone up all the boys you fancy and arrange a date with a different boy on every day of the week!
3. Insist that your big sister takes you out on the town with her and her mates!
4. Take up martial arts, so you can spend one evening a week grabbing boys and wrestling them to the ground!!
5. Buy a very large box of fattening chocolates and invite the girls round for a mega pig-out!!!

WHY IT'S BETTER TO BE SINGLE!

Yus, stay on your own and smile!

1. You don't have to fork out for expensive birthday/ Christmas presents!
2. You don't have to stand in the freezing cold and rain on a Saturday afternoon watching him play football!
3. You don't have to put up with another set of parents!
4. If you've not got a boyfriend, you won't be jealous at Christmas parties when all the boys are busy trying to snog every girl there!
5. You'll have lots of time to work on your novel (ahem!)!

And Makin' Up!

Some may say this is the best part of an argument! You can be subtle about makin' up or totally over the top! Let's take a look, shall we?

HOW TO PERSUADE HIM TO MAKE UP!

How could he resist this little lot?!

1. Plant a very large kiss on his lips when he's not expecting it!
2. Cry at his feet!
3. Pay some carol singers to go round and sing outside his house while you give him a snog!
4. Send him a bundle of soppy records tied up in a big pink ribbon!
5. Phone him up and tell him how much you love him! Aaaw!

GREAT WAYS TO SAY YOU'RE SORRY

Go on — swallow your pride!

1. "Oh, Honeykins, I'm so sorry! Please forgive me!"
2. "I've missed you a lot and my teddy's fed up of being cuddled, can I have the real thing?!"
3. "I've missed your lips, baby!"
4. "Nothing's worthwhile if I can't have you with me to share it." (Spew!)
5. "Come here!" At this point you should grab his lapels and snog his face off!

GREAT PLACES TO DO YOUR MAKIN' UP!

Forget the back row of the cinema! Do it true romance style!!

1. In the middle of a downpour — he'll look sooo cute with raindrops dripping off his nose!
2. Outside your front door in the moonlight where you had your first snog together!
3. In front of all the people who smirked when you fell out!
4. In the middle of the park when it's snowing!
5. At the end of the disco when the slow records are playing!

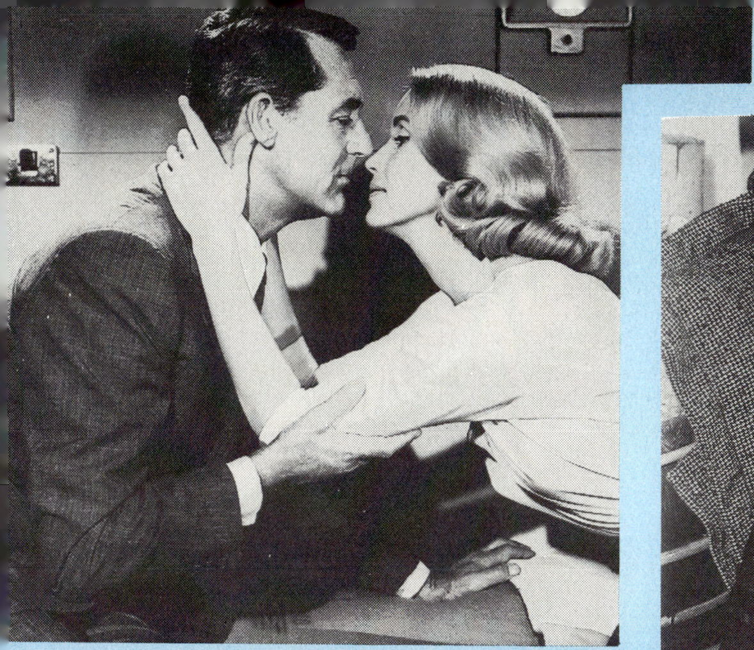

WHY IT'S FUN TO BE GOING STEADY!

Mmm, snogs and cuddles and lots more!

1. If you're feeling bored you can lift the telephone and demand to be entertained.
2. There's snogs whenever you want them!
3. You've aways got someone to dance with at the disco!
4. There's someone to cuddle up to when you're watching a scary film!
5. Creeps will think twice about pestering you for a date!

Check out these classic hunks — sigh, they just don't make 'em like this anymore!

NAME: TONY CURTIS (real name Bernie Schwartz!!)

BORN: NEW YORK, 1925

IN-DEPTH INFO: After leaving the Navy in 1944, Tony decided to take drama lessons and this led to him being signed up by a large film company (Universal) and he started his career on screen! He went on to star in fab films like 'Some Like It Hot' with Marilyn Monroe (he said kissing her was like kissing a man!), and 'The Vikings'. Between all this he married Janet Leigh, who was the unlucky woman in the shower in 'Psycho', and became a dad when Jamie Lee was born! In the 70's he made a TV series with Roger Moore called 'The Persuaders'. Nowadays, Tony has fetching white hair and a pot belly and likes to be seen with young models!

TRY TO SEE HIM IN:

'The Prince Who Was A Thief'
'The Hustler'
'Son Of Ali Baba'
'The Square Jungle'
'The Vikings'
'Some Like It Hot'

CLASSIC CRUMBLIES

NAME: TYRONE POWER

BORN: CINCINATTI, 1913

IN-DEPTH INFO: Tyrone's mom and pop were in the entertainment business so when he was a nipper Tyrone made up his mind what he wanted to be — an actor! In 1932 he landed a few "bit parts" in flicks called 'Tom Brown Of Culver' and 'Flirtation Walk'. He moved to Hollywood and appeared in a "host" of films and married a French actress called Annabella. In 1939 he found himself more popular than Clark Gable and Spencer Tracy! Sadly towards the end of the 40's his films became pretty awful and he decided he wanted to go back to Broadway but his bosses at the studio said no, so poor Tyrone was forced to make some more rather dodgesome movies. By 1953 his contract was "up" with the studio and he legged it to London to appear on stage. He died in 1958 in Madrid after filming a fight scene.

TRY TO SEE HIM IN:

'Girls Dormitory'
'Jesse James'
'Johnny Apollo'
'The Mark of Zorro'
'The Black Swan'
'Rawhide'
'Solomon and Sheba'

NAME: CLARK GABLE

BORN: OHIO, 1901

IN-DEPTH INFO: Before Clark made women's hearts melt, he was a lumberjack in his home town of Cadiz! He moved to New York and "trod the boards" in a number of plays! His first screen performance was in a western called 'The Painted Desert' in 1931. He appeared in about 20 films up until 1940 when along came the big one — 'Gone With The Wind'!! This secured Clark as a major heart-throb! Even now, more than 50 years on, females everywhere swoon at the sight of Rhett Butler! It's because of this part, that the hunky Mr Gable is still as much of a pin-up today!

In 1942, he shocked the movie world by enlisting for the army. In between all this going on, Clark had managed to get himself hitched three times (tragically, his third wife, actress Carol Lombard, was killed in a plane crash). His first two wives had been somewhat older than himself! He married a further two times and had a son — Clark Gable Jnr. In 1961 he starred alongside Marilyn Monroe in 'The Misfits' which was his very last movie as he died a few weeks after filming finished.

TRY TO SEE HIM IN:

'Mutiny On The Bounty' — the first one!
'Sporting Blood'
'Laughing Sinners'
'The Possessed'
'Boomtown'
'Betrayed'
'Teacher's Pet' — with Doris Day
'Gone With The Wind' — of course!

NAME: FRANK SINATRA

BORN: NEW JERSEY, 1915

IN-DEPTH INFO: Old Blue Eyes is, as they say, a "living" legend. He started his career as a singer and had girls everywhere a' swoonin' with his croonin'! It wasn't long before Frank was snapped up to do his stuff in films. He won an Oscar for his performance in 'From Here To Eternity' and went on to star in films like 'Guys And Dolls', 'High Society' and most "noteably" 'The Cannon Ball Run'. (?)

When Frank was a mite younger he could count Marilyn Monroe and Grace Kelly amongst his girlfriends!

TRY TO SEE HIM IN:

'Ship Ahoy'
'Anchors Aweigh'
'Step Lively'
'From Here To Eternity'
'Ocean's Eleven'
'The Manchurian Candidate'
Why not listen to some of his "toons" as well?!

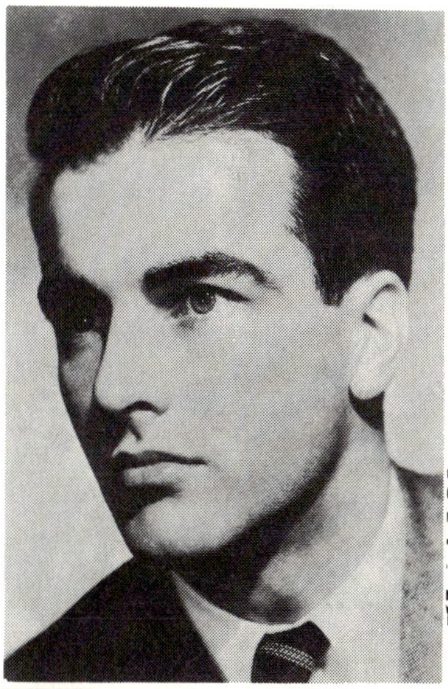

NAME: MONTGOMERY CLIFT

BORN: NEBRASKA, 1920

IN-DEPTH INFO: Montgomery Clift's life was a fairly sad one. He started off an angel of the silver screen and ultimately became a burned-out alcoholic by the age of 45. He made his film debut in 'Jubilee' in 1935 and over the next few years starred alongside the likes of John Wayne and Marilyn Monroe. It was a film called 'From Here To Eternity' that really put him on the pinnacle of success. He won his third (and last) Oscar for his portrayal of a victimised GI hero. Sadly his career took a step backwards over the next couple of years. He never married and started to drink heavily towards the end of his life, in 1966.

TRY TO SEE HIM IN:

'Sunset Boulevard'
'From Here To Eternity'
'A Place In The Sun'
'I Confess'
'The Misfits'

NAME: STEVE McQUEEN

BORN: MISSOURI, 1930

IN-DEPTH INFO: Young Steve ran off to join the Marines when he was just a teenager and decided to "jump ship" in New York. He was at a bit of a "loose end" so he attended drama school for four years. Broadway payed his wages for the next few years until his debut in 'Never Love A Stranger'. Next came a part in 'The Blob'! Steve went on to star in such classics as 'The Great Escape' and 'Bullitt'. He insisted on doing all his own motorbike stunts and had a passion for racing cars. He married actress Ali McGraw and sadly died in 1980.

TRY TO SEE HIM IN:

'The Magnificent Seven'
'Never So Few'
'The Honeymoon Machine'
'The Great Escape'
'Nevada Smith'
'The Thomas Crown Affair'

NAME: MARLON BRANDO

BORN: NEBRASKA, 1924

IN-DEPTH INFO: Big 'n' beefy Marlon was a real wild child as he was expelled from military academy at 15! He decided to shift to New York where he appeared on Broadway for a few years and appeared in the stage version of 'A Streetcar Named Desire'. He was spotted by a director and snapped up to appear in a film called 'The Men' in 1950. But it was in 1951 Brando really shot to fame — he made the movie of 'A Streetcar Named Desire' and won some hefty awards. He shocked everyone by turning up at posh functions wearing jeans and a T-shirt! Shocka!!! In 1954 he made a film called 'The Wild One' which was a tale about two rival motorbike gangs and was banned in Britain for 12 years! A few years later he shed his bad boy image (in the movies anyway!) to appear in the musical 'Guys And Dolls' with Frank Sinatra! He went on to win an Oscar for 'On The Waterfront' and he actually wore a suit to the ceremony!

Marlon was married twice and now lives with a woman called Tarita who he met while filming 'Mutiny On The Bounty'!

Nowadays Marlon is a portly old soul and we've not seen much of him since the fabulous 'Godfather'!

TRY TO SEE HIM IN:

'A Streetcar Named Desire'
'Julius Caesar'
'The Wild One'
'On The Waterfront'
'Mutiny On The Bounty'
'Superman' — he got a whopping one million bucks for appearing for 10 minutes at the beginning!
'The Godfather'

NAME: PETER O'TOOLE

BORN: EIRE, 1933

IN-DEPTH INFO: One of the few remaining wild men of the movies, Peter started life as a journalist on his local newspaper but chucked it in and got a place in RADA. He toured the country in plays and met his first wife Sian Phillips. His first movie role was in 1959 where he played a Scotsman in 'Kidnapped'. Then along came his most memorable performance, Lawrence in 'Lawrence Of Arabia'.

He was a bit of a hellraiser and was oft' seen out on the town with his good friend Richard Burton! He then went on to star in the likes of 'What's New Pussycat' and 'Goodbye Mr Chips'! Most recently you've probably seen him in 'High Spirits' where he was wild and wrinkly. He's still going strong!

TRY TO SEE HIM IN:

'Lawrence Of Arabia'
'Lord Jim'
'What's New Pussycat'
'The Lion In Winter'
'Great Catherine'
'Murphy's War'

NAME: ERROL FLYNN

BORN: TASMANIA, 1909

IN-DEPTH INFO: Errol had a rather exciting life before he stepped in front of the cameras! He was a gold hunter, a diamond smuggler and a policeman!! His first movie was in 1934 called 'Murder In Monte Carlo' and he followed it up with 'The Case Of The Curious Bride'. Errol had a bit of a naughty reputation which was fuelled somewhat when he was caught snogging one of the lady guests at HIS wedding reception! He came within inches of playing Rhett Butler in 'Gone With The Wind', but found out that Bette Davis was up for the part of Scarlett, and since they hated each other, they both pulled out! He had a rather "full" life which included many women, drinks and parties! It all proved too much and Errol died in October 1959 aged 50.

TRY TO SEE HIM IN:

'Charge Of The Light Brigade'
'The Adventures Of Robin Hood'
'The Private Lives Of Elizabeth And Essex' (With his "good friend" Bette Davis!!)
'They Died With Their Boots On'
'The Adventures Of Don Juan'

NAME: PAUL NEWMAN

BORN: OHIO, 1925

IN-DEPTH INFO: No doubt your mum will be swooning as well! Paul's one of the gentlemen of Hollywood and has been in the "business" for 40 years now!

In 1947 he moved to Illinois and ended up appearing on a TV show called 'The Aldritch Family' and making movies for TV.

Over the next 10 years he appeared in heaps of movies including 'Cat On A Hot Tin Roof', 'Butch Cassidy And The Sundance Kid' and 'The Hustler'.

He's been married to actress, Joanne Woodward for over 30 years and now has his own range of salad dressings!!

TRY TO SEE HIM IN:

'The Hustler'
'Torn Curtain'
'Colour of Money' — with Tom Cruise
'Cool Hand Luke'
'Butch Cassidy And The Sundance Kid'

NAME: JAMES DEAN

BORN: INDIANA, 1931

IN-DEPTH INFO: There isn't much you can say about James Dean that hasn't been said before! The ultimate in rebels and pin-ups! He was only 24 when he died in a car accident, but had managed to make three mega movies! In reality he was always a bit of a loner and while dating Ursula Andress was prone to "shoving her about a bit". Even though he's been dead for over 30 years he's still got the appeal and following he had when he was alive.

TRY TO SEE HIM IN:

'East Of Eden'
'Rebel Without A Cause'
'Giant'

Head

Keep your locks chic and shining with these happenin' hairdos!

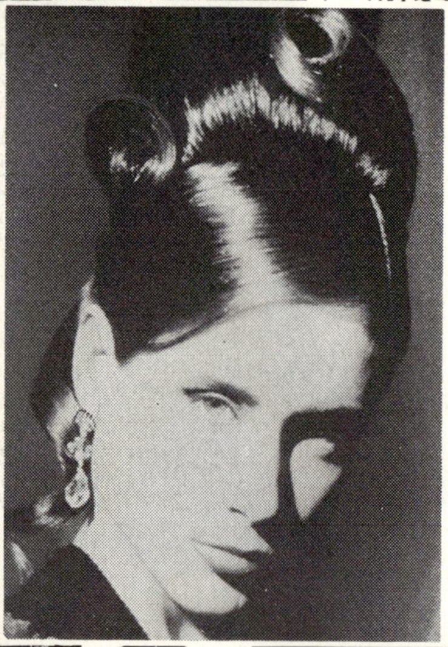

by Guy Kremer for Schwartzkopf

L'Oreal using "Grafic" products

Taylor Ferguson (Salon) Glasgow

L'Oreal using "Grafic" products

Lines!

by Anthony Mascolo for Schwartzkopf

L'Oreal using "Studio Line" products

L'Oreal using "Studio Line" products

by Charlie Miller for Schwartzkopf

by Sarah for Vidal Sassoon

THE GROOVY MOVIE

SPOT THE SOUNDTRACK!

Who provided the interesting background noise to the following films . . .
a) 'Batman'
b) 'Great Balls Of Fire'
c) 'Working Girl'
d) 'Homeboy'
e) 'Buster'

HUGHES THE BOSS!

In the 80's, the most famous movie-maker for teen films was undoubtedly John Hughes, so see if you can answer a few teasers based on his films!
a) Who played rowdy rebel John Bender in the 1985 hit 'The Breakfast Club'?
b) Which English group recorded the theme tune to the Molly Ringwald masterpiece 'Pretty In Pink'?
c) Steve Martin didn't have his troubles to seek in 'Planes, Trains and Automobiles', but who was the "portly" gent who made his travelling even worse?
d) Who provided the voice to John Travolta's baby in 'Look Who's Talking' last year?
e) Can you name the yuppie couple who try to settle down in 'She's Having A Baby'?

FILM FEMME FATALES

A quick section on the many girls on film.
a) She was brilliant in 'Beetlejuice', happening in 'Heathers' and great in 'Great Balls Of Fire'. Who is she?
b) A dangerous liaison with a certain Baron Munchausen set this girl up for stardom, so can you name her?
c) Which moonchild had to choose between James Spader and Dexter Fletcher in 'The Rachel Papers', but had Keanu Reeves all to herself in 'River's Edge'?
d) In which film did Lisa Bonet make her movie debut as mystical Epiphany Proudfoot?
e) What do Page Hannah, Annabeth Gish, Phoebe Cates and Bridget Fonda have in common?

DEAD PARROTS' SOCIETY!

70's mirth makers turned 80's movie makers — the Monty Python team are now producing some of Britain's funniest films. Are you Monty mad?
a) In which 1989 film did John Cleese play one of a team of bungling medieval Scandinavian warriors?
b) 'A Fish Called Wanda' contained two Monty Python actors — who were they?
c) Which fairy-tale was written and directed by Python Terry Gilliam and starred ex-Monty Eric Idle as the fastest man on earth?
d) Name the South American country which gave its name to a film containing many a Monty Python member.
e) The Monty Python team's version of biblical events caused quite a stir — can you remember what it was called?

QUIZ

What do you know about the movie world and its many inhabitants? Find out if you're a film boffin in this easy-peasy bright 'n' breezy quiz!

TELLY ADDICTS!

Many movie stars originally found fame and fortune on television, but how much do you know about them?

a) He started off as David Addison in 'Moonlighting' but went on to star in the films 'Blind Date', 'Die Hard', 'Sunset' and 'In Country', who is he?
b) Where was Tom Selleck's detective series 'Magnum P.I.' based?
c) This hippy-head started off his acting career in a series called 'Seven Brides For Seven Brothers', who is he?
d) Which director originally appeared as Ritchie Cunningham in 'Happy Days' and then went on to mastermind 'Cocoon', 'Willow' and 'Parenthood'?
e) Name Michael J. Fox's business-like character in 'Family Ties'.

ACT UP!

Name the musicians who starred in these films . . .

a) 'Scandal'
b) 'Stormy Monday'
c) 'Lost Angels'
d) 'Shanghai Surprise'
e) 'Dogs In Space'

ROUND UP ON RIVER!

How much do you know about Mr Phoenix, the man who put the "toff" in tofu? Well, you're about to find out!

a) Which British comedienne did River star alongside in 'I Love You To Death'?
b) Where was River born, and in which year?
c) Name the two films in which he starred next to Harrison Ford.
d) Can you name River's three sisters and one brother?
e) For which film was Mr Phoenix nominated for a Best Supporting Actor Oscar?

LOVE ON A MOVIE SET

Match up the movie stars who are also off-screen "chums".

1) Dennis Quaid	**a) Martha Plimpton**
2) Kevin Kline	**b) Tracy Pollan**
3) Bruce Willis	**c) Meg Ryan**
4) River Phoenix	**d) Phoebe Cates**
5) Michael J. Fox	**e) Demi Moore**

COMIC CINEMA

What can you remember about the films that made you chuckle all the way home?

a) Which film contained Charlie Sheen, Tom Berenger and Corbin Bernsen as members of a team of baseball misfits?
b) Who were 1989's Dirty Rotten Scoundrels?
c) Name the character that Tom Hanks played in the body-swap classic 'Big'.
d) Before he cleaned up Gotham City, in which film did Michael Keaton play a ghoulish exorcist?
e) Which Beatles "number" did Matthew Broderick/ Ferris Bueller serenade an ecstatic crowd with on his "day off"?

MIX UP!

Unscramble the letters to find five of the best.

a) I CHARM YOE
b) O SIR ME CUT
c) CAT RIP WAZ KEYS
d) CUB WILLER SIB
e) VARU SEEKNER

ANSWERS

SPOT THE SOUNDTRACK!
a) Prince or Danny Elfman
b) Jerry Lee Lewis
c) Carly Simon
d) Eric Clapton
e) Phil Collins.

HUGHES THE BOSS!
a) Judd Nelson
b) The Psychedelic Furs
c) John Candy
d) Bruce Willis
e) Elizabeth McGovern and Kevin Bacon.

FILM FEMME FATALES
a) Winona Ryder
b) Uma Thurman
c) Ione Skye
d) 'Angel Heart'
e) They all starred in 'Shag'.

DEAD PARROTS SOCIETY!
a) 'Erik The Viking'
b) John Cleese and Michael Palin
c) 'The Adventures of Baron Munchausen'
d) 'Brazil'
e) 'The Life Of Brian'.

TELLY ADDICTS!
a) Bruce Willis.
b) Hawaii
c) River Phoenix
d) Ron Howard
e) Alex P. Keaton

ACT UP!
a) Roland Gift.
b) Sting.
c) Ad-Rock/Adam Horowitz.
d) Madonna.
e) Michael Hutchence.

ROUND UP ON RIVER!
a) Tracey Ullman
b) Madras, Oregon in 1971
c) 'The Mosquito Coast' and 'Indiana Jones and The Last Crusade'
d) Rainbow, Summer, Liberty and Leaf.
e) 'Running On Empty'.

LOVE ON A MOVIE SET!
1) Dennis Quaid — c) Meg Ryan
2) Kevin Kline — d) Phoebe Cates
3) Bruce Willis — e) Demi Moore
4) River Phoenix — a) Martha Plimpton
5) Michael J. Fox — b) Tracy Pollan

COMIC CINEMA
A) 'Major League'
b) Michael Caine and Steve Martin
c) Josh Baskin
d) 'Beetlejuice'
4) "Twist And Shout".

MIX UP!
a) Corey Haim
b) Tom Cruise
c) Patrick Swayze
d) Bruce Willis
e) Keanu Reeves

CONCLUSIONS

41-50

Well, we didn't know Barry Norman bought the Jackie annual! Congratulations, you fully deserve the title of Film Buff Of The Year, in fact you probably know the name of the "key grip" or "best boy" on 'Batman'! The only problem is, you'll annoy your friends and irritate your family if you constantly wander about saying things like, "Did you know Robert Downey Jnr's first acting role was as a puppy?!" Anyway, hearty congrats, and treat yourself to a massive tub of popcorn!

21-40

Mmm, not bad, you certainly have a passing knowledge of things cinematic but you'd probably prefer a night at the disco to a night at the Cannon! The next time you're moaning about being bored, pop out to your video shop or take a trip to the pictures, you never know — you might even enjoy it! Until then, look back over past issues of Jackie and start swotting!

0-20

Dear oh dear oh DEAR! Movies aren't exactly your strong point, are they? Oh well, I'm sure you find more interesting hobbies to pursue, such as the washing-up, homework or cleaning up the budgie cage! Spend your next weekend hiring the entire filmography of Tom Cruise, Rob Lowe and Molly Ringwald from your video shop, or risk being a movie mincehead for the rest of your life!

JACKIE
MATT DILLON
SHOT: RETNA

SECOND BEST?

Lee really liked Diane, but she already had a boyfriend . . .
IT'S NO USE! I DON'T STAND A CHANCE WITH DIANE WHILE SHAUN'S AROUND — SHE'S GOT NO TIME FOR ANYONE ELSE!

. . . BUT YOU SAID THAT LAST WEEK AND THE WEEK BEFORE, SHAUN. YOU WON'T STAND ME UP, THIS TIME, WILL YOU?
'COURSE NOT! IT'S THE OPENING OF THAT NEW CLUB IN TOWN — I WOULDN'T MISS IT FOR ANYTHING!

I DON'T KNOW WHY YOU BOTHER WITH HIM, DIANE! HE'S LET YOU DOWN SO MUCH, LATELY!
BUT HE COULDN'T HELP THOSE NIGHTS HE DIDN'T TURN UP, SUE. HIS MUM WAS ILL . . .
YEAH, THAT'S WHAT HE TOLD YOU! THE LEAST HE COULD HAVE DONE WAS PHONE YOU. I RECKON YOU COULD DO BETTER THAN SHAUN.

HI, LEE. YOU GOING TO THE DISCO, TONIGHT?
I DON'T KNOW YET, SUE. HI, DIANE. ARE YOU GOING TO THE DISCO WITH SHAUN TONIGHT?
MAYBE — IF HE REMEMBERS TO TURN UP!

I WONDER WHAT SHAUN'S UP TO, CHATTING TO THAT GIRL? I HOPE HE ISN'T GOING TO DO THE DIRTY ON DIANE. SHE DESERVES MUCH BETTER THAN HIM . . .

BUT, LATER THAT NIGHT . . .
THAT'S SHAUN WITH ALISON WATTS AND IT LOOKS AS IF THEY'RE GOING OUT FOR THE NIGHT! HE MUST HAVE STOOD UP DIANE AGAIN!

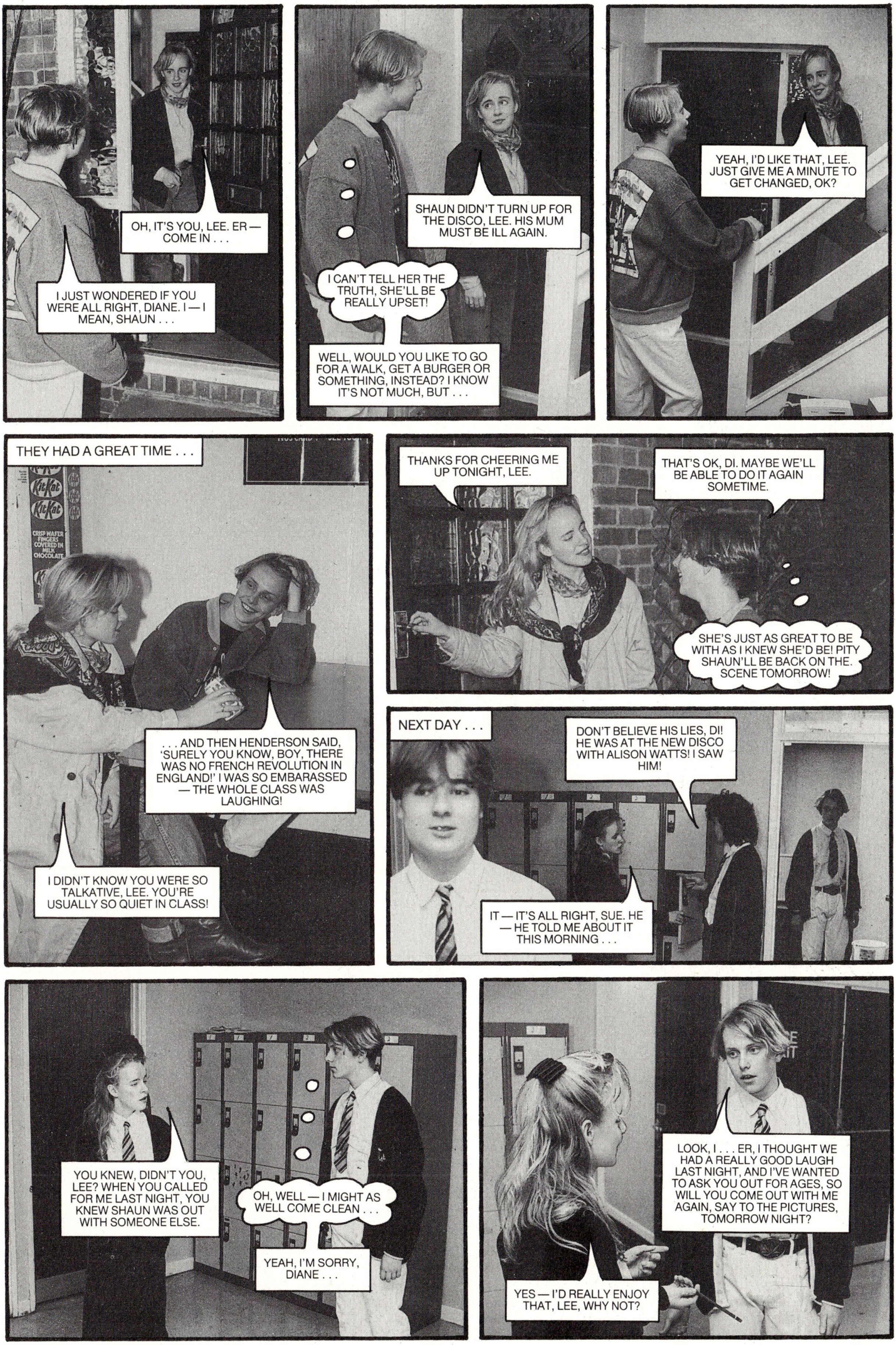
OH, IT'S YOU, LEE. ER — COME IN . . .
I JUST WONDERED IF YOU WERE ALL RIGHT, DIANE. I — I MEAN, SHAUN . . .
SHAUN DIDN'T TURN UP FOR THE DISCO, LEE. HIS MUM MUST BE ILL AGAIN.
I CAN'T TELL HER THE TRUTH, SHE'LL BE REALLY UPSET!
WELL, WOULD YOU LIKE TO GO FOR A WALK, GET A BURGER OR SOMETHING, INSTEAD? I KNOW IT'S NOT MUCH, BUT . . .
YEAH, I'D LIKE THAT, LEE. JUST GIVE ME A MINUTE TO GET CHANGED, OK?
THEY HAD A GREAT TIME . . .
KitKat
KitKat
CRISP WAFER FINGERS COVERED IN MILK CHOCOLATE
. . . AND THEN HENDERSON SAID, 'SURELY YOU KNOW, BOY, THERE WAS NO FRENCH REVOLUTION IN ENGLAND!' I WAS SO EMBARASSED — THE WHOLE CLASS WAS LAUGHING!
I DIDN'T KNOW YOU WERE SO TALKATIVE, LEE. YOU'RE USUALLY SO QUIET IN CLASS!
THANKS FOR CHEERING ME UP TONIGHT, LEE.
THAT'S OK, DI. MAYBE WE'LL BE ABLE TO DO IT AGAIN SOMETIME.
SHE'S JUST AS GREAT TO BE WITH AS I KNEW SHE'D BE! PITY SHAUN'LL BE BACK ON THE SCENE TOMORROW!
NEXT DAY . . .
DON'T BELIEVE HIS LIES, DI! HE WAS AT THE NEW DISCO WITH ALISON WATTS! I SAW HIM!
IT — IT'S ALL RIGHT, SUE. HE — HE TOLD ME ABOUT IT THIS MORNING . . .
YOU KNEW, DIDN'T YOU, LEE? WHEN YOU CALLED FOR ME LAST NIGHT, YOU KNEW SHAUN WAS OUT WITH SOMEONE ELSE.
OH, WELL — I MIGHT AS WELL COME CLEAN . . .
YEAH, I'M SORRY, DIANE . . .
LOOK, I . . . ER, I THOUGHT WE HAD A REALLY GOOD LAUGH LAST NIGHT, AND I'VE WANTED TO ASK YOU OUT FOR AGES, SO WILL YOU COME OUT WITH ME AGAIN, SAY TO THE PICTURES, TOMORROW NIGHT?
YES — I'D REALLY ENJOY THAT, LEE, WHY NOT?

FOR THE NEXT FEW WEEKS . . .
THEY SAW A LOT OF EACH OTHER . . .
AND . . .
YOU LOOK MUCH HAPPIER THESE DAYS, DI. I TOLD YOU YOU COULD DO BETTER THAN SLIMY SHAUN, DIDN'T I?
YES, LEE *IS* NICE . . .
BUT . . .
I CAN'T HELP BEING SCARED SHE STILL FANCIES SHAUN, AND *HE* CERTAINLY FANCIES HER!
THE FOLLOWING WEEK AT THE DISCO . . .
ENJOYING YOURSELF, DI?
I ALWAYS DO NOWADAYS, LEE, THANKS TO YOU!
HEY, GUESS WHAT? ALISON'S PACKED SHAUN IN! SERVES HIM RIGHT FOR TWO-TIMING YOU, EH, DI?
ER, YES. IS THAT FOR ME, SUE? I'M DYING OF THIRST!

I WISH HE'D STOP STARING AT HER! IT'S OBVIOUS WHAT HE'S THINKING! I SUPPOSE IT'S ONLY A MATTER OF TIME BEFORE HE ASKS HER OUT AGAIN . . . JUST MY LUCK . . .
ARE YOU OK, LEE? YOU'RE VERY QUIET TONIGHT.
FINE, THANKS, DI. JUST THINKING, THAT'S ALL . . .
SHE ONLY WENT OUT WITH ME 'COS HE DIDN'T WANT TO KNOW, AND NOW, I'VE GOT THIS AWFUL FEELING. SHE WAS CRAZY ABOUT SHAUN . . . WHAT CHANCE HAVE I GOT WHEN HE TRIES TO ELBOW HIS WAY IN AGAIN . . ?
LOOK, I REALLY MEAN IT, DIANE — JUST GIVE ME ANOTHER CHANCE . . .
SHAUN, I . . .
COMING TO THE CANTEEN, DI? OH — SORRY . . .
HANG ON A MINUTE, LEE. WHERE'RE YOU GOING?
TO THE CANTEEN. I DIDN'T THINK YOU'D WANT TO COME.
WHY? 'COS I WAS TALKING TO SHAUN? LOOK, LEE, YOU MIGHT AS WELL KNOW, HE WAS ASKING ME TO GO BACK WITH HIM . . .
WELL, I GUESSED THAT WOULD HAPPEN . . .
HE ASKED ME, AND I SAID NO. *YOU'RE* MY BOYFRIEND NOW, AND THAT'S THE WAY I WANT IT TO STAY, OK?
YOU REALLY MEAN IT?
OF COURSE, I DO! SHAUN'S JUST A TWO-TIMING RAT — I COULD NEVER TRUST HIM AGAIN!
I COULDN'T HAVE PUT IT BETTER MYSELF!
THE END

WORKING ON IT!

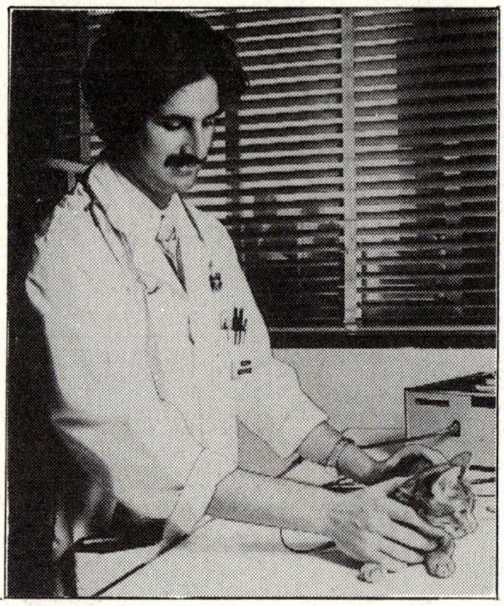

VETERINARY

INVOLVES: Looking after and attending to the general health of animals, livestock and/or pets. All aspects of welfare covered— operating, treatment with drugs — handling all types of animals from next door's cat to a farmer's prize bull. Work can be physically demanding as strength is required to handle larger animals and can also be a 24 hour job.

QUALIFICATIONS: A degree in veterinary medicine. For entry to university, you will need 5H grade passes or 3 A level passes, all at grades A or B. Competition is VERY stiff.

YOU'LL LIKE IT IF:
- You're genuinely interested in animals (i.e. not overly sentimental about them)
- You like the idea of working outdoors
- You need a challenge (no two days are the same in a vet's life!)
- A 9 to 5 job would drive you mad!

YOU'LL HATE IT IF:
- You look on animals as being "cute" or "cuddly"
- You need a set routine
- You can't stand the sight of blood
- You're nervous or scare easily
- You go to pieces under pressure.

NURSE

INVOLVES: Care of those who are physically/mentally ill/handicapped which includes washing/feeding, giving medication, monitoring conditions and following doctor's instructions. Work can be messy and sometimes distressing.

QUALIFICATIONS: 2 A levels or 3 highers for degree courses and you must be at least 17½ years old.

YOU'LL LIKE IT IF:
- You genuinely care about people
- You have a sympathetic nature
- You don't mind personal commitment
- You can communicate well with people.

YOU'LL HATE IT IF:
- You go to pieces in a crisis
- You get easily upset
- You don't like working in a team
- You don't have any common sense!

JOURNALIST

INVOLVES: Reporting, writing articles for publication, correcting grammar and spelling, cutting work to an acceptable length. Also involved is thinking up ideas for features, supervising photo-sessions, covering local events and interviewing people.

QUALIFICATIONS: A Pre-Entry Course in journalism studies or training on the National Council of Journalists' scheme. Often entry to a junior position doesn't require these but they do help. Entry usually requires 2 A levels or 3 highers including an A/B pass in English.

YOU'LL LIKE IT IF:
- You enjoy writing
- You're enthusiastic and outgoing
- You like meeting people
- You don't like the idea of being stuck at a desk!

YOU'LL HATE IT IF:
- You're shy
- You're not very creative
- You can't work under pressure
- You're totally disorganised!

So, you want to be . . . a journalist, a vet, an engineer. What qualifications do you need? How do you know if you'll like it? What's involved? Well, it's all here — read on and find out!

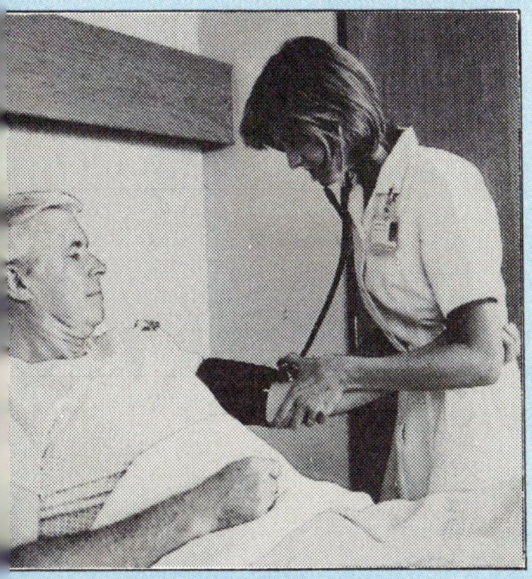

HAIRDRESSER

INVOLVES: Reception work, making appointments and answering phone. Advising customers on styles, suggesting various changes, shampooing, cutting, perming, colouring/tinting, blow drying and styling. Juniors start off by sorting towels, sweeping and cleaning up, doing reception work and making coffee.

QUALIFICATIONS: No formal requirements but exam passes may be required for college courses. Check with the college you're interested in.

YOU'LL LIKE IT IF:

- You enjoy working with people
- You're interested in fashion and appearance
- You like working with your hands
- You don't mind working long hours.

YOU'LL HATE IT IF:

- You find it difficult to concentrate
- You can't communicate with people
- You don't like the idea of working on a Saturday
- You'd rather be sitting at a desk!

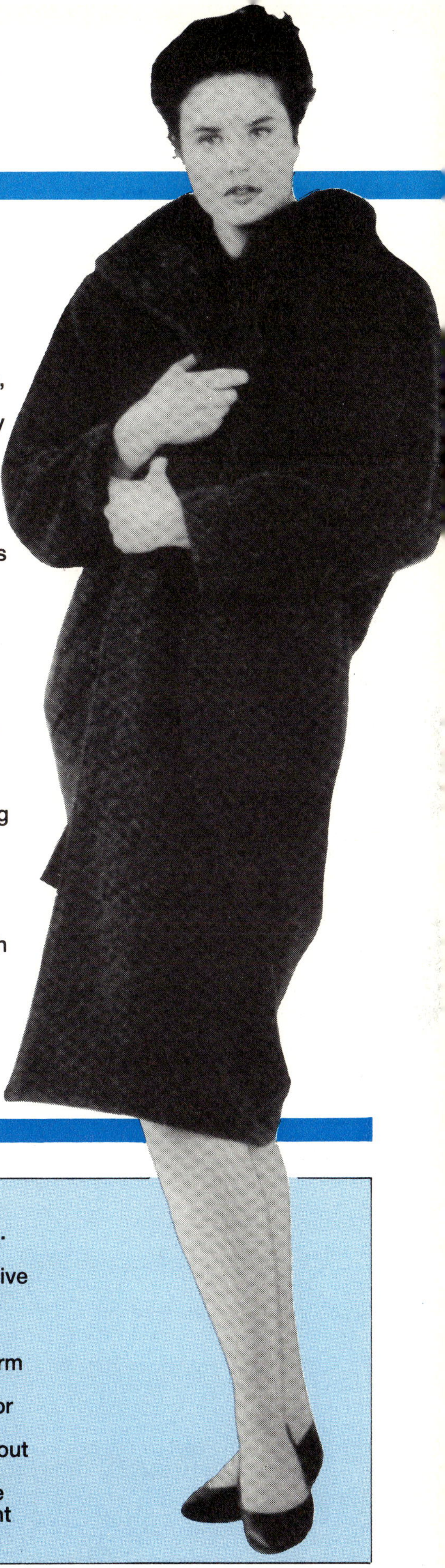

MODEL

INVOLVES: Working in a studio or on location for magazines or mail order catalogues. A few may be good enough to work on "catwalk" for high fashion and designer shows.

QUALIFICATIONS: None, although a good basic education is an advantage. Training is mainly via experience. Must be at least 5'8" and have good physical features; skin, teeth, hair and be well-proportioned.

YOU'LL LIKE IT IF:

- You're relatively outgoing.
- You're punctual
- You're inventive/imaginative
- You can accept criticism.

YOU'LL HATE IT IF:

- You'd like to work in a warm office (location work and conditions can be cold/hot or cramped/uncomfortable)
- You couldn't care less about your appearance
- You'd rather go out on the town than have an early night
- You don't like travelling.

TRAVEL AGENT

INVOLVES: Selling travel/holidays to the public. This means taking details, deposits, arranging hotel accommodation and giving advice on different types of holidays. Also involves filling in booking forms, recording payments and issuing tickets.

QUALIFICATIONS: A foreign language is a big advantage but various courses vary in their requirements.

YOU'LL LIKE IT IF:
- You're interested in travel
- You're well organised
- You have an outgoing and friendly personality
- You can interpret what a customer wants.

YOU'LL HATE IT IF:
- You couldn't care less about travel!
- You're totally scatter-brained!
- You don't like using the phone.
- You don't like dealing with the general public.

SCIENCE

There are so many categories in this field it would be impossible to list them all, so we've chosen civil engineering as an example.

CIVIL ENGINEER

INVOLVES: Working on and monitoring construction projects, deciding where to build, what materials to use, how much it'll cost, manpower involved and machines required in mechanics and aerodynamics of structures. Also oversee projects including staff and finances and involved in design of buildings, dams, roads, etc.

QUALIFICATIONS: Usually a degree which needs 2-3 A levels or 3-4 highers — usually physics and maths. Colleges normally have their own requirements.

YOU'LL LIKE IT IF:
- You enjoy a challenge
- You have a logical/mathematical mind
- You're interested in science
- You have a technical understanding.

YOU'LL HATE IT IF:
- You can't stand maths or physics
- You find it difficult to concentrate
- You don't like outside work
- You don't like the idea of shift work.

CONTACTS

Banking Information Service,
10 Lombard Street,
London
EC3V 9AT.

Engineering Careers Information Service,
54 Clarendon Road,
Watford,
Herts
WD1 1LB.

Hairdressing Training Board,
17 Silver House,
Silver Street,
Doncaster,
S. Yorks
DN1 1HL.

National Council for the Training of Journalists,
Carlton House,
Hemnall Street,
Epping,
Essex
CM16 4NL.

London College of Fashion (for info. on modelling),
20 John Princes Street,
London
WIM 0BJ.

National Board for Nursing,
22 Queen Street,
Edinburgh
EH2 1JX.

The Institute of Travel and Tourism,
113 Victoria Street,
St. Albans,
Herts
AL1 3TJ.

Royal College of Veterinary Surgeons,
32 Belgrave Square,
London
SW1X 8QP.

When writing to any of the addresses listed, please enclose a stamped, addressed envelope.

BANK CLERK

INVOLVES: Dealing with the general public, sorting cheques, obtaining balances and account details, buying and selling currency, arranging traveller's cheques and dealing with queries.

QUALIFICATIONS: Preferably 2 A levels or 3 highers but individual banks will have their own requirements for their training schemes.

YOU'LL LIKE IT IF:
- You're interested in money and finance
- You can organise and plan things
- You don't mind responsibility
- You think you can deal with staff and customers in difficult situations.

YOU'LL HATE IT IF:
- You're not very tactful
- You don't like responsibility
- You have little or no patience
- You don't work well in a team.

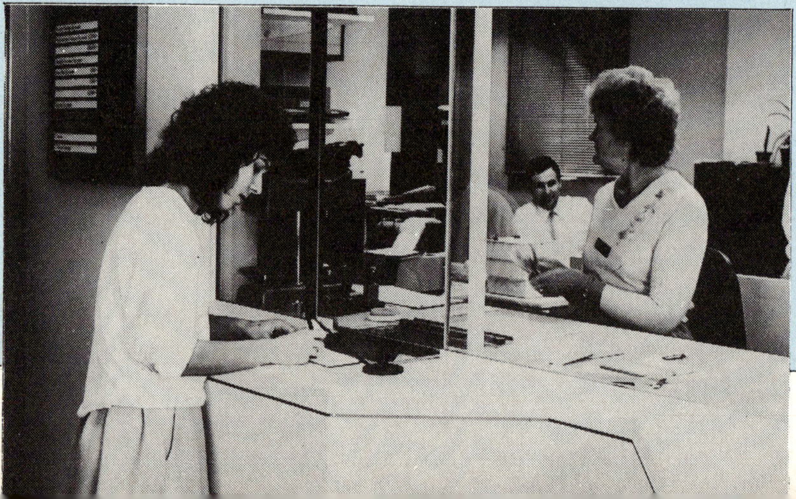

PAH! Goody-two-shoes! Don't they make your blood boil?! Or maybe you're one yourself!! We take a look at some real 'butter-wouldn't-melt-in-their-mouths' types and try not to pull their pigtails!

GOODY TWO-SHOES!

GOODY GOODY GIRLS!

Get your plateful of "mom's" apple pie ready, and take a look at some of the goodiest-two-shoes ever!!

DORIS DAY — She's the star of all the good girls, who else would wear a "blouse" like that?!

DEBBIE GIBSON — It's hard to imagine the American songstress doing anything bad, isn't it?

CARON KEATING — Just the fact that she was a 'Blue Peter' presenter says it all about Caron — squeaky clean and no mistake!

WHITNEY HOUSTON — Just an overgrown Girl Guide really!

ANNIE JONES (Jane from 'Neighbours') — Aaah, poor little Jane! With a granny like Mangel it's no wonder she's not got much "go" in her!

MAVIS FROM 'CORONATION ST.' — Too boring to be anything else but well-behaved!

BONNIE LANGFORD — The creature with the shrill voice and red hair who never grew up! Bonnie looks and acts about 12 years old! Spew!

ANNEKA RICE — All blonde hair, teeth and girlish giggles!

SARAH GREENE — Sarah's got a permanent smile and is always sooo nice to everyone on 'Going Live'! Even her "better half" Mike Smith is a birrova goody-goody!

GOODY GIRLS ON FILM!

'THE BREAKFAST CLUB' — Molly Ringwald (herself a goody-goody) plays a very "uppity" young madam in this John Hughes classic! Lovely pink sweaters, ahoy!

ABSOLUTELY ANY DORIS DAY FILM!!! — No matter what part she played, Doris always came across as the ultimate in goody-two-shoes!

'DANGEROUS LIAISONS' — The film was v. raunchy, but dainty Michelle Pfeiffer was sickeningly sugar sweet all through!

'PRETTY IN PINK' — Good ol' Molly Ringwald again, whose ultimate ambition is to go to the prom — eek!

'GREASE' — Ah, the old favourite! Olivia Newton John playing the ultimate 'Miss Prim'. The songs were good though!

'SHAG' — Phoebe Cates is a champion goody to start with but soon becomes a raver towards the end! Hurrah!

THINGS 'GOODIES' NEVER DO!

Kiss on the first date!
Wear jeans more than once a week!
Put on too much lipstick!
Read saucy novels!
Come home late from the movies!
Hand their homework in late!
Go out with scruffy boys!
Listen to Guns N' Roses.
Fight with their family!
'Bunk off' school!
Jump a queue!

QUIZ...QU

OK, would butter melt in your mouth?! Shall we find out?

1

1. Yeah! Your mum and dad are going away for the weekend and leaving the house in your charge! All your friends are suggesting that you have a party — what do you do?

a) Get on the telephone right away to everyone you've ever met and tell them to get round to your house to party, pronto!!
b) Invite a few friends round to watch some videos but keep it quiet and send them home at midnight!
c) You would never dream of having a party while your parents were away! Things could get broken and someone always spills Um Bongo on your mum's white rug!

THINGS THAT 'GOODIES' LIKE!

Going to their school 'prom'!
Phillip Schofield!
Home-baking!
Fluffy teddy bears!
Organising dances and things!
Chatting to their teachers after class!
Visiting their granny on a Sunday afternoon.
Spoiling people's fun!
Boys who wear sensible shoes!

GOODY TWO-SHOES TOGS!

A goody's ideal wardrobe!

Nice frilly blouses!
Anything that's pink!
Home-knitted cardigans!
Long nightdresses!
Sensible shoes!
Hat and scarf sets!
Fluffy slippers!
Warm 'anoraks'!

Z...QUIZ...QUIZ...

2. It's the school Christmas party and someone suggests that you ask your grumpy old maths teacher to dance! Do you:
a) drag him onto the dance floor and deliberately stand on his toes,
b) ask him to dance, but wait until it's an Iron Maiden record so he's left clueless in the middle of the dance floor,
c) ask him to dance to the Military Two Step and impress him with your dancing skills?!!

3. Your luck is in, because your big brother and his mates have said that they don't really mind if you tag along with them to an all-night party!! His friends are all hunks — what do you do?!
a) Have your make-up and little black dress on in five seconds flat!
b) Say you'll go but insist someone brings you home for 11 o'clock.
c) Refuse point blank to go! All-night parties are a bit risqué and if your parents found out they'd kill you!

4. There's a new disco just opened up in your town and everyone is going! Your mum says that you've got to stay in and do some studying! Pah! What do you do?
a) Climb out your bedroom window and zoom right on over to the disco!
b) Try to reason with your mum by telling her you'll study twice as hard tomorrow night!
c) Realise that your mum's only thinking of you and get your pens and pencils ready for a night of books and learning?!

5. You're on a school holiday in France! Everyone's decided that they're going to sneak out of the hotel at midnight and go to a disco!! It's risky but fun, do you join in?
a) Of course! You'll lead the way, you're not about to miss out on all those French boys!
b) You're a "trifle" scared but you'll go along with it anyway, as it could turn out to be quite a giggle!
c) Absolutely not! It's a stupid idea and if you get caught it'll ruin the holiday as you'll all get grounded!

MOSTLY A'S

Ho, ho! You're certainly a little "tearaway" aren't you?! You're definitely not a member of the "goody gang"! There's no pigtails or frilly blouses for you and you wouldn't dream of behaving yourself! Tut! Go and lock yourself in your bedroom and don't expect any supper!!

MOSTLY B'S

Well we wouldn't expect to see you at every single party or disco that's being held, but you'd probably make an appearance at a few. You're not a goody two-shoes, just "sensible"! The minute you get an urge to take up home baking, be careful — it's the first sign!

MOSTLY C'S

You really are sugar and spice and all things nice, aren't you? You would never dream of doing anything naughty and are never happier than when you're doing your sewing! Lighten up a little, and that doesn't mean playing your records a little louder than usual — though we bet you think that's pretty wild, huh?!!

DOUBLE ACTS!

MARIA

KENNETH

MARIA

Make-up
Maria has lovely clear skin so Vivienne went for a very light honey foundation with some loose powder dusted over for a smooth finish. A light dusting of tawny blusher added colour. Vivienne then brushed a muted pink shadow up to the eyebrows with a burnt brown shadow blended into the socket. A smudge of soft brown pencil along with a coat of brown-black mascara added definition. A soft sugary brown lipstick was applied for totally "tasty" kissers.

Hair
Maria has very, very, long hair which Vivienne twisted and pinned up into a "messy" top knot with a few long wispy bits left loose and twirly for a "sophisticated" look.

KENNETH

Make-up/Hair
Although he doesn't normally wear the stuff, Kenneth consented to a wee dollop of powder to even out his skintone. After that a blob of hair wax was slicked into the old barnet and that was that!

Our make-over girlies asked us if it was OK to bring along their "men" to see if we could get them out of their jeans and into something a bit more . . . em . . . "attractive"! So we gathered hundreds of smart items and whisked the whole lot of 'em off to be transformed by our make-up artist and the rest of the make-over crew — and here they are!

SHARON

LINDSAY

SHARON

Make-up

Sharon has very fair skin, so Vivienne applied a wee dot of pale porcelain foundation with a light dusting of matching powder and a dot of dusky rose blusher for an "English Rose" look!

A pale russet shadow was brushed up to her eyebrows and a mushroom shadow blended into the socket and under the lower lashes. A brown mascara was added to her already very long lashes. To complete the look Vivienne applied a sweet iced honey lipstick.

Hair

Sharon has natural blonde hair with a perm so Vivienne pinned back the side sections and twirled the fringe for a soft, feminine style.

LINDSAY

Hair/Make-up

A mere dot of tinted moisturiser was applied to Lindsay's skin to even it out and add a bit of a "healthy glow"! Some hair wax was carefully applied with a few strands getting special attention for a "sculptured look"!

CONTINUED ▶

DOUBLE

KENNETH

Clothes

Green trousers, a green wool jacket and a posh shirt and he was transformed into one totally cool "dude"!

MARIA

Clothes

For a long, lean, luscious look we went for a cropped velvet jacket with high-waisted velvet pants and chunky earrings.

SHARON

Clothes

To show off just how tiny Sharon is, we plumped for a black top with gold brocade and matching harem pants and a few shimmery, shiny jewels!

LINDSAY

Clothes

A pair of dark green trousers and a "colourful" shirt made one rather handsome "chap"!

THE VERDICT

"It's been great fun and we've all enjoyed it — thanks!"

ARIES

Direct, sporty and street-wise, you need someone with lots of get up and go to stop you feeling dead bored! You fall in love mega fast but then lose interest just as quickly if things get too heavy! Moody signs like *Cancer* and *Scorpio* leave you cold but *Leo's* a great partner for your fiery temper and bubbly personality. Lively *Sagittarius* is THE best match of all for an exciting romance that's anything but dull!

TAURUS

You should avoid flirty signs like *Gemini* and *Sagittarius* who only cause you loads of bother and bags of sleepless nights! Watch out for sultry *Scorpio* to set those pulses tingling, but don't expect it to last too long (you're both mega bossy!). *Capricorn* and *Virgo* suit your down-to-earth nature. They can just about handle your stubbornness and bring lots of romantic times together!

GEMINI

Flirty, flighty and good fun, romance is just one big game to you! You're easily bored and when a love-affair shows a hint of going stale (or getting too deep), you head straight for the door! Avoid possessive partners like *Leo* or *Scorpio* who want to get serious much too soon! Look for lively times with *Aquarius* and for a more serious fling, charming *Libra* could be your Mr Right!

CANCER

You lurve being in love, but find it hard to say goodbye when a romance is coming to an end. Cool on the surface, underneath you're an emotional little girlie. Signs like *Aquarius* and *Gemini* just don't understand your deep feelings and cause lots of pain, but sensitive *Pisces* and passionate *Scorpio* are fellow water signs who suit you right down to the ground.

YOUR PERFECT

LEO

Passionate, outrageous and determined, you hate being told what to do and need loads of freedom to go your own way. Romance means fun, but signs like *Libra* or *Aquarius* should stand clear, 'cos if your pride's hurt you'll never forgive them! *Aries* and *Sagittarius* make great mates while *Pisces* gives loads of love AND let you have ALL the limelight you think you deserve!

VIRGO

Miss Super Cool — critical and down to earth (but just a bit shy too) you know exactly what you want. The problem is NO-ONE seems to match up to be your perfect partner! *Taurus* and *Capricorn* are the signs you can rely on and surprise, surprise, *Aries* can bring loads of good times too!

LIBRA

Easy-going and charming, you soon have everyone eating out your hand! The problem is you take so long to make a decision, the boys just give up waiting for that date! Lighthearted and romantic, you enjoy the company of *Libra* and *Aries* but need possessive signs such as *Taurus* and *Cancer* like a hole in the head! *Aquarius* is the one who understands you need lots of freedom and bags of time to make ANY decision!

SCORPIO

Phew — intense, sultry and mysterious, your magnetic appeal soon has the boys running in your direction. But your moodiness turns signs like *Libra* or *Sagittarius* into quivering wrecks! Only water signs like *Pisces, Cancer* or another *Scorpio* can handle your deep emotions and give you ALL the love you need. And if they don't, no-one is as great as you for planning SPECTACULAR revenges!

SAGITTARIUS

You hate being tied down and need plenty of space. Loads of friends are often more important than passionate romance! *Cancerians* and *Scorpios* are just MUCH too possessive and you can't break free from their grip to have all the fun you need! *Aries* understands you have to have lots of freedom and elusive *Aquarius* keeps you interested and well and truly on the hop!

CAPRICORN

Super cool, ambitious and practical you may be, but underneath you just long for real romance. When you fall in love (and that takes ages), you go head over heels, so need someone who won't let you down. *Aries* and *Libra* drive you to distraction 'cos they're so unreliable, but *Virgo* and *Taurus* are always around when you need a shoulder to cry on.

AQUARIUS

Detached, aloof and impassive, your quiet appearance hides a quick mind and a need for lots of independence. *Taurus, Scorpio* and *Leo* all attract you, but then try to boss you around, and that's the surest way to make you say goodbye! Fun-loving *Sagittarius* and chatty *Gemini* understand your need for lots of breathing space and just love it when you speak your mind and tell THEM what to do!

PISCES

Easy-going and dead soppy, you spend hours writing poetry and slushy love songs! But when a relationship's over, you're just too sensitive to tell and drift away into the distance! *Virgo* and *Sagittarius* find you attractive and *Gemini* thinks you're cool but SO indecisive. *Scorpio* and *Cancer* understand every emotional bone in your body while *Leo* is the big romantic you just can't resist!

PARTNER... IT'S IN THE STARS!

ARIES
SAGITTARIUS

Jon (New Kids On The Block), Don Johnson, Andrew McCarthy, Kiefer Sutherland, Judd Nelson.

TAURUS
CAPRICORN

Nathan Moore (Brother Beyond), Joe (New Kids On The Block), Jason Connery.

AQUARIUS
LIBRA

Matt and Luke (Bros), Sting, Brian Ferry.

CANCER
SCORPIO

Ralph Macchio, Mags Furholmen (a-ha), Nick Thorpe (Curiosity), Simon le Bon.

LEO
PISCES

Rob Lowe, Jon Bon Jovi, Bruce Willis, Terence Trent D'Arby.

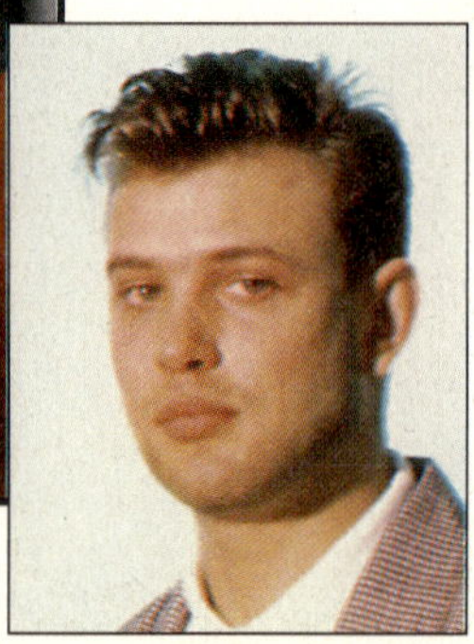

VIRGO
TAURUS

Ben Volpeliere – Pierrot (Curiosity), Danny and Jordan (New Kids On The Block), Emilio Estevez, Bono.

GEMINI

AQUARIUS

Matt Dillon, Michael Hutchence.

SCORPIO

CANCER

Tom Cruise, George Michael, Jim Kerr, Marti Pellow (Wet Wet Wet).

SAGITTARIUS

ARIES

Jon Cryer, Simon Climie, Phillip Schofield.

CAPRICORN

VIRGO

River Phoenix, Charlie Sheen, Morten Harket (a-ha), Michael Jackson.

LIBRA

GEMINI

Jason Donovan, Roland Gift, Michael J. Fox, Prince.

PISCES

LEO

Patrick Swayze, Sean Penn, Donnie (New Kids On The Block).

ARE YOU A POP TOFF?!?

Well, you'd better be 'cos we've got a mega pop quiz for you! Put on your thinkin' caps and settle down to three pages of teasers . . !

MUSCLE MEN

Mmm, muscles . . . but who's got the best?

1. Which hunky muscle man appeared (briefly) in 'Ghostbusters II'?
2. Who bared his chest in many an episode of 'Neighbours', then again in 'Heroes'. Pwwoooargh!
3. Who's the not-so-hunky one in Wet Wet Wet?
4. Who are the hunky brothers in New Kids On The Block?
5. Which Goss twin was a labourer before super-stardom?

AROUND THE COUNTRY

Aaah, the British Isles, they've spawned many a star, but who exactly?

1. He's incredibly hairy, he's a glamorous grannie's sex symbol and he's from Wales . . . but who is he?
2. Which country did Simple Minds and Texas spring to life in?
3. Which area in London were the Goss twins born in?
4. Which Scottish group named themselves after hearing a line in the Scritti Politti song, "Getting, Having And Holding"?
5. Which Irish group does Bono front?

WHO SAID WHAT?

What utterings came from which stars' mouths?

1. "There's a bit on my tummy to the right of my belly button which absolutely kills me. If someone tickles me there, it's the worst thing ever!"
2. "I've got the hairiest toes you've ever seen! Right by the nail, I've got long bushy bits . . . but I've often had praise heaped upon me for my small ears."
3. "I think she's *gorgeous*. She looks so lovely." And all this about Kylie!!
4. "Three times now we've declared war on a hotel. This involves heavy artillery, terrorist attacks . . . an all out assault on the hotel, all its inhabitants and workers, ha-ha!"
5. "We had a chat and he was sweet and I gave him my phone number and he said he'd call me next time he was in town. But I've never gone on a date with Bobby Brown!"

DYNAMIC DUOS

Duos — don't ya just love them? Well, we sure do, but do you know who these "splendid" twosomes are . . ?

1. This pair are related and they were born on September 29th 1968 in Lewisham, South London.
2. They've been hailed as style "gurus", and they've worked with Liza Minnelli and Dusty Springfield. Who are they?
3. They first appeared in 1985 with an album called "Pale Shelter", then they reappeared in 1989 with "The Seeds Of Love" — who are they?
4. What very dynamic duo dance in "roomy" trousers and big black boots and live in Hamburg?
5. Where do Milli Vanilli call home?

TERRIFIC TRIOS

Three's not always a crowd — here're some threesomes we all love . . !

1. You'll all know their first names, but what about their surnames? Who are Prestwick, Gillespie and John better known as?
2. Which female group did Siobhan Fahey sing with before turning into a sister of Shakespear?
3. Which trio is fronted by a Gift?
4. They're Norwegian, they've all got funny names, they're . . . who?
5. Which group crooned with crinkly Diana Ross way back in her "hey-day"?

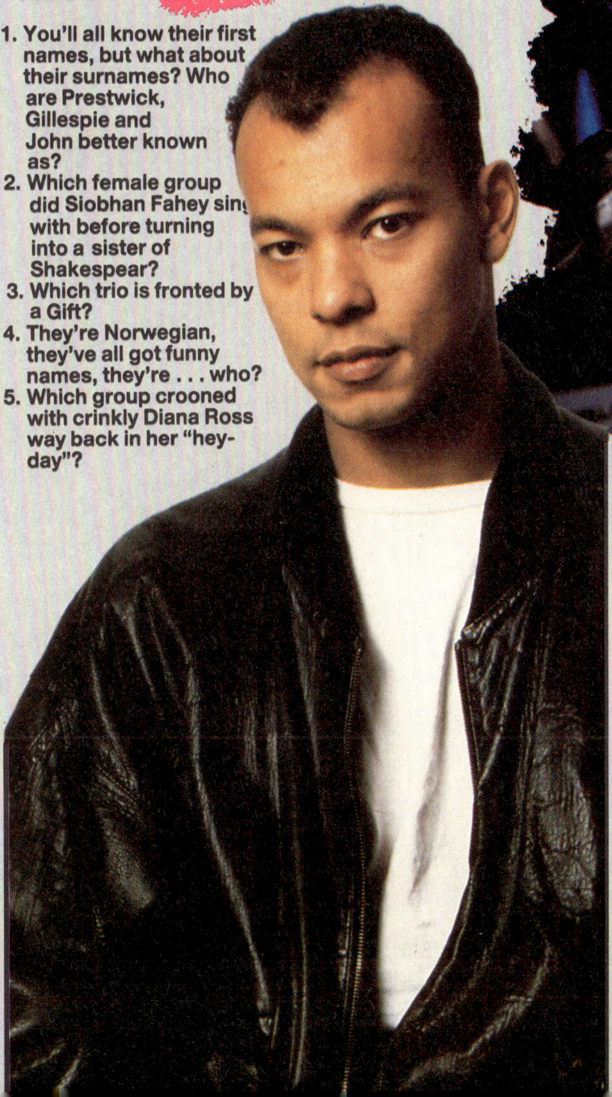

PRANCIN' DANCERS

Get on your dancin' feet and tiptoe through the teasers . . .

1. Which "triffic" dancers are also known as Dennis and Edem?
2. What did Jason, Mark and Phil "blame" it on?
3. Which girl danced with Prince before going off to do her own "thang"?
4. Who's the youngest member of the all-dancin', all-singin' New Kids On The Block?
5. Who danced and sang her way to fame in American shopping malls?

OLDIES BUT GOLDIES

Aah, the good old crumblies . . . where would we be without them?

1. Who celebrated his 100th single in 1989 and is still "going strong"?
2. Who made his big screen debut in 'Buster'?
3. Who's the cute crumblie who gave us Kylie, Jason, Sonia and a whole "host" of stars?
4. Which ex-Beatle lives in the Mull of Kintyre and churns out singles with his wife, Linda?
5. Which band does Freddie Mercury sing with?

FIRST HITS

Who had their first hits on these shores with these fab "toons" . . ?

1. "You Got It (The Right Stuff)"
2. "Nothing Can Divide Us"
3. "Wishing I Was Lucky"
4. "When Will I Be Famous"
5. "Really Saying Something"

continued overleaf

FIRST LADIES

Pop vixens and songstresses are the bees knees, but do you know all the "gen"?

1. What was Kylie's first number one in Britain?
2. What's Madonna's full name?
3. What leggy lovely was a model then a stylist for Wham?
4. Was Sinitta born in Britain or America?
5. Which band is Wendy James the lead singer of?

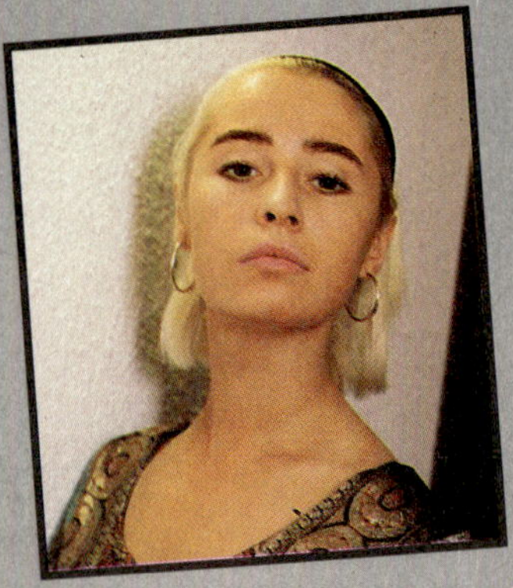

VITAL STATISTICS

Pop "stars" are renowned for their weird and wonderful shapes, but, for now we think we'll content ourselves with the height of these lovelies . . !

1. How many inches separate the top of Kylie's head from the soles of her feet?
2. How tall (or small) is Adeva?
3. How many feet and inches do Bros share?
4. Is Jason Donovan 5′ 4″, 5′ 11″ or 6′ 1″?
5. Who's the tallest member of Big Fun?

THE ANSWERS!!!

MUSCLE MEN
1. Bobby Brown
2. Jason Donovan
3. Tommy Cunningham
4. Jon and Jordan Knight
5. Luke

AROUND THE COUNTRY
1. Tom Jones
2. Scotland
3. Lewisham, South London
4. Wet Wet Wet
5. U2

WHO SAID WHAT?
1. Matt Goss
2. Nathan Moore
3. Michael Hutchence
4. Donnie Wahlberg (New Kids)
5. Martika

DYNAMIC DUOS
1. Matt and Luke Goss
2. Neil and Chris — Pet Shop Boys
3. Tears for Fears
4. Dennis and Edem — The London Boys
5. Holland

TERRIFIC TRIOS
1. Phil, Mark and Jason of Big Fun
2. Bananarama
3. Fine Young Cannibals
4. a-ha
5. The Supremes

OLDIES BUT GOLDIES
1. Cliff Richard
2. Phil Collins
3. Pete Waterman
4. Paul McCartney
5. Queen

PRANCIN' DANCERS
1. The London Boys
2. The Boogie!
3. Cat
4. Joe McIntyre
5. Tiffany

FIRST HITS
1. New Kids On The Block
2. Jason Donovan
3. Wet Wet Wet
4. Bros
5. Bananarama

FIRST LADIES
1. "I Should Be So Lucky"
2. Madonna Louise Veronica Ciccone
3. Yazz
4. Seattle, USA
5. Transvision Vamp

VITAL STATISTICS
1. 5′ 1″
2. 6′ 1″
3. 6′ 1″ (12′ 2″ if you add them together!)
4. 5′ 11″
5. Phil Prestwick

THE CONCLUSIONS!!

0-33 Ahem, what can we say, you're not exactly a pop "toff", are you? You'll never get on in the "biz" that way, will you? Smarten up with a few of Jackie's "superb" pop pages and do better next time, OK?!

34-66 Mmm, not too bad, but you could still do better, couldn't you!? Dig out your pop encyclopedias and get your nose stuck in!

67-100 You've done so well, you must've cheated! No, seriously, you're pretty sharp on the old pop "gen", aren't you?! And we thought we'd set a hard test too, huh! We'll get you next time, matey!!

JACKIE
MARTI PELLOW
SHOT: SIMON FOWLER

AND SO TO BED...

BED TIME SHOULD BE FUN! THROW AWAY THOSE OLD T-SHIRTS AND BATTERED JIM-JAMS AND STEP INTO SOMETHING DIFFERENT. BRIGHTEN UP YOUR ROOM WITH WACKY ALARM CLOCKS AND CUDDLY BEARS . . . WHO WANTS TO GROW UP ANYWAY?!

"HELLO? . . HELLO?!!! IS THAT THE SPEAKING CLOCK?!"

SNOOPY PYJAMAS, FROM ETAM. TELEPHONE SLIPPERS, FROM SAXONE. MULTI-COLOURED ALARM CLOCK, FROM BHS. POLAR BEAR, AND PANDA & BABY BEAR, BOTH FROM LITTLEWOODS.

"MORNING AEROBICS NEVER LOOKED SO GOOD!"

FLUFFY ROMPER SUIT, FROM ETAM.

Photographer: MIKE DAVIS

CONTINUED ▶

AND SO TO BED...

"OHH TO BE GLAMOROUS!!"

ROBE, FROM THE FREEMANS CATALOGUE (STYLE NO. UN4204). BOXERS, FROM THE FREEMANS CATALOGUE (STYLE NO: UK5208). BRA, (PART OF SET) FROM TOP SHOP.

"I'M OFF FOR A SHOWER WITH TEDDY."

EXTRA LONG TOWELLING ROBE, AND TEDDY PYJAMAS, BOTH FROM ETAM. PASTEL TEDDY BEAR, FROM LITTLEWOODS.

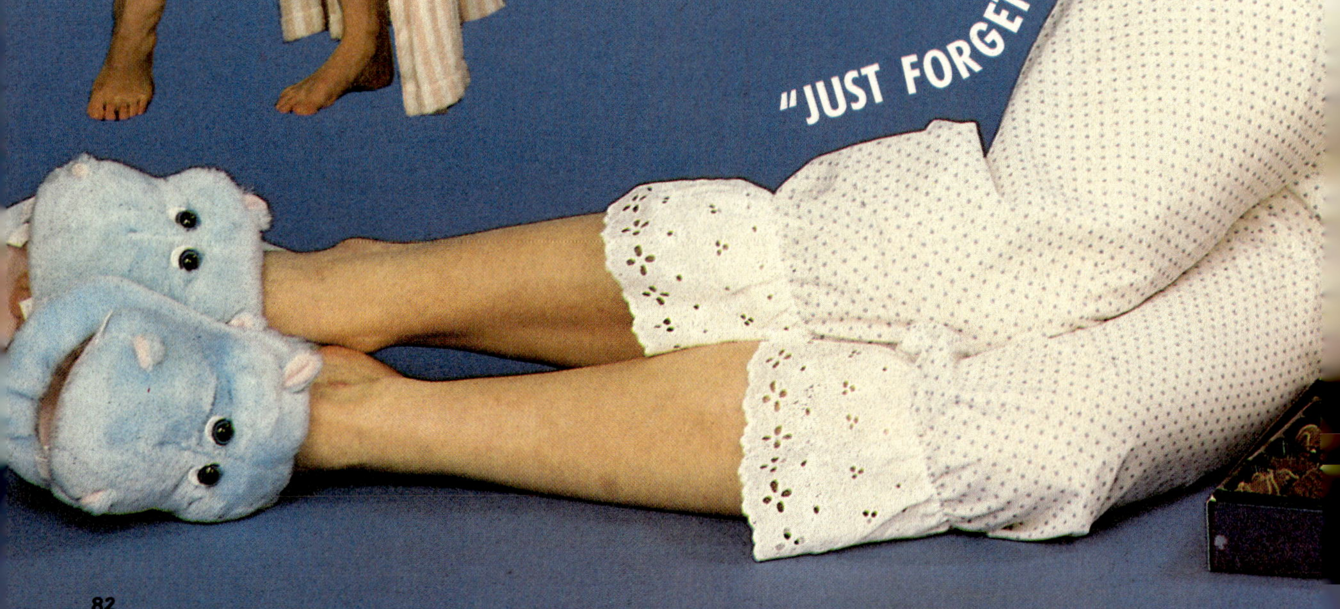

"JUST FORGET THE CALORIES!!"

SPOTTY ROBE, AND PYJAMAS, BOTH FROM LITTLEWOODS. ALARM CLOCK, FROM BHS.

HIGH NECK ALL-IN-ONE, AND FLORAL PRINT PYJAMAS, BOTH FROM HENNES.

CAMISOLE TOP PYJAMAS, FROM THE FREEMANS CATALOGUE (STYLE NO: UG5237). BLUE HIPPO SLIPPERS, FROM FREEMAN HARDY WILLIS. SMALL PINK ALARM CLOCK, PINK HEART CUSHION, AND WATER BOTTLE COVER, ALL FROM LITTLEWOODS. COPPER LOOK ALARM CLOCK, FROM BHS. FLUFFY MOOSE SLIPPERS, FROM FREEMAN HARDY WILLIS. BIARRITZ CHOCOLATES, BY CADBURYS.

Kath had arranged everything — all Jenny had to do was knock him for six!

BLIND DA

SHORT STORY BY MELISSA MITCHESON-LEE.

TE

GUESS WHAT?" Kath came bursting into my bedroom looking like she'd just won the pools!

I looked up from my magazine. "What?"

"Well, call me a genius because that's just what I am!" she said smugly.

"Oh, yeah?" My sister's always full of mad schemes that never quite come off. This was going to be another one, I just knew it. I went back to my magazine, trying to give her as little encouragement as possible.

"Kate, listen to me!" she demanded. "I've only gone and got you fixed up with David Hammond, haven't I?"

"What?" Immediately she had my full attention.

"See." She grinned. "I knew you'd be impressed."

I gulped. "David Hammond? Oh, Kath!"

She shrugged. "It was nothing. I collared him in the canteen at lunchtime. 'Dave,' I said, 'Dave, I have this incredibly sexy looking sister and —' "

I threw the magazine at her. "Come on! Tell me what really happened."

"I'm telling you, aren't I? I've fixed you up — tomorrow, around six."

"I just don't believe this!" I said, retrieving my magazine and hoping she wouldn't notice my red face.

"Well you'd better. And don't you let me down! This could be your big break!"

And then she was off, to have a bath and glam herself up for Paul Lewis, who she's killing time with till the tall, dark and handsome man of her dreams whisks her away.

My big break . . . she wasn't kidding. David Hammond. I couldn't take it in. I'd heard all about him from Kath, of course, when she'd started working at the estate agents. I'd seen him once or twice, driving off in his flash red sports car when I'd gone to meet her after work. But never in my wildest dreams had I imagined something like this.

"Mum!" I yelled, hanging over the banister. "Mum! Is my blue skirt clean?" I had to start getting ready now! No time to waste.

"HOW DO I LOOK?"

I dreamed about David Hammond all night, and by the following afternoon I was in a right old panic.

"How do I look?" I asked Kath. She was sprawled out on my bed, scoffing the last of the Jaffa Cakes. I stood sideways on in the mirror, holding my stomach muscles in. "Well?"

She grinned up at me, swallowed and brushed crumbs all over the bedspread. "Awful, one look and he'll run a mile!"

"Thanks a lot!" I let my muscles go again, peered in the mirror and smudged on a bit more lippy. Then I wiped it off again. I had to look just right — *perfect* — this was the most important date of my life. "This top OK?"

Kath nodded. "Yes, it's fine — honest. Stop worrying."

I sank down on to the bed beside her. "Kath, what if he doesn't like me? What if I walk through the door and he thinks — YUCK?"

"Don't be a twit! Look, I've told him all about you — he wouldn't have wanted to meet you if he didn't like the sound of you, would he?"

I sighed, pulled on my jacket and said, "I suppose not."

But I had butterflies all the same. Kath had done this sort of thing loads of times before, but it was the very first time for me. She'd been threatening to fix me up for ages, but I never thought she'd really do it. Now it was actually happening, I was like a jelly.

"I don't know what to say, Kath," I said. "I don't know how to act, what to do . . ."

"Let him do most of the talking," Kath said. "And just — be yourself."

"Yeah," I agreed, as a last look in the mirror confirmed that no amount of mascara was going to transform me into a Vogue model. Maybe he didn't rate them anyway. Kath was right — I'd have to turn up as me, and if he didn't like what I was, well . . . it would be his loss, wouldn't it?

HE was even groovier looking close up. A classic hunk — dark hair, dark eyes. When he smiled, his whole face lit up.

"How about a coffee?" he asked.

My butterflies did somersaults. "Er — yes, thanks."

"Let's sit over here," he said, pointing at a couple of spare seats.

"Right," I said, following him across the room. I felt as if the other people there were all staring at me. I swallowed. I kept swallowing. I was sure I'd smudged my make-up running for the bus.

"You've just left college, haven't you?" His voice was really deep, it sent ripples up my spine.

I swallowed again. "Yes — er . . ." My voice didn't sound like my voice at all. Anyway, he probably thought he was wasting his time already. I knew I wasn't as good looking, or as clever as Kath. Why would he want to meet someone like me? No doubt Kath made me sound a lot more interesting than I am. Why couldn't I be more like her?

He handed me a cup of coffee. I didn't dare try to pick it up, though, my hands were shaking so much. "What were you doing at college, then?" he asked. He really seemed to want to know, as if he was interested in what I said.

"Oh, you know, secretarial, and all that . . ." And then suddenly it was easy. Suddenly I seemed to know what to say to him. even made him laugh once or twice, when I told him about Mrs Marshall and the shorthand classes.

"What do you want to do now you've done your exams and everything?" he said eventually.

And I found myself telling him about my ambitions (even if they weren't very big ones), talking over my hcpes and plans. Even telling how I wanted to save up and go to Greece, like Kath did last year. How I didn't just want to be a typist, how I'd like to be on reception somewhere I could meet people . . .

THE TIME HAD FLOWN BY.

He listened to me as if I were the most important person in the world. Taking in every word.

And he was funny, too. Telling me about his job, the people he met, the places he went. I looked at my watch and realised we'd been talking for ages. I couldn't believe it. The time had flown by.

"Well, it's nice to have met you," he started saying, looking at his watch, too.

"Yes . . ." I felt awkward again. I didn't know if I should just get up and go, or what. Surely, *surely,* he wasn't going to leave it at that? I stood up. "I — um — suppose I'd better go . . ." Why didn't he say something? I thought he liked me . . . was he just being polite?

He stood up, too. Smiled. So I smiled back — hopefully.

He took my hand then, and all the butterflies that had been asleep suddenly leaped up and started dancing round my stomach again.

"Congratulations," he said. "You've got the job."

ILLUSTRATION: JACKY ROUGH.

TRACY
SUPERDRUG "SCRUNCH" RANGE (FROM 79P)

Styling Wax

This has a rather pleasant odour — it's a bit like raspberries, actually! It's OK but a bit too greasy for me. 2/5.

Styling Mousse

Not quite "super wild" as it claims but not bad all the same. There was no mention of it being ozone friendly which is a bit suspect! 2/5.

Styling Gel

Definitely "strong hold" stuff this — a winner. 4/5.

Style 'n' Fix Spray

Keeps every strand in place — and it's ozone friendly. 5/5.

Apart from the wax they all smell a bit too chemically. They'd overpower any perfume you wore! They all work pretty well, though, and they're dead cheap!

TRACEY
WELLA "SHOCKWAVES"

Mousse

The mousse wasn't really my cup of tea! It smells awful and tended to make your hair sticky. 2/5.

Gel

Much better! Not too "gluey" and lasted for ages. 4/5.

Hairspray

Pretty good! Your hair won't budge after a few scooshes and it'll keep it in place all night! 5/5.

KAREN
SCHWARZKOPF "NEWS"

The rather "mean 'n' stylish" packaging caught my eye immediately. Would the contents be just as exciting?

Fixing Spritz

Alas, no! The Fixing Spritz was the most disappointing of the bunch. The directions on the bottle were very vague, so I tried it on both wet and dry hair. It gave a fairly firm hold, but my hair felt "crispy" and very sticky to touch — not something you'd want to run your fingers through! 2/5.

Wax

This is a nice, squishy, un-sticky wax which was easy to warm up in my hands and apply. It would probably be best for short, slicked back styles as it's quite soft and gives your hair a "sheen". (Or, as someone who shall remain nameless said to me, your hair looks greasy!) It depends on your point of view! 3/5.

Conditioner

Mmm! This had a wondrous, but not overpowering smell and it left my hair fairly soft and shiny, too. What more can you say? 4/5.

What they are and how to use 'em!

WAX

This is a splendid product that's actually been around in one form or another for a long time. It's usually hard (or at least firm) to the touch and you only need a teensy weensy bit otherwise you'll end up with very greasy hair! Take a small blob and warm it in your hands till it's quite soft. Apply sparingly! It's great for sculpting long strands and curls and adds loads of shine and style to short hair.

MOUSSE

This is great for scrunchy styles and it adds volume to fine hair without making it sticky or heavy. Use a blob about the size of a golf ball, hang your head upside down and apply it to the roots and down to the ends. Make it messy by drying upside down or comb the mousse through for a sleek finish.

GEL

Gels are great for short spikey styles, scrunchy messy locks, and sculpting a few strands. Don't use too much as it'll go hard and horrible. Apply to the roots for volume or slick it back for a cool style.

FIXING SPRAY

This is like hairspray but it can also be used on wet hair. Great for sculpted styles — use before and after to keep it rock hard. Go for the pump action variety for more precision.

PAULINE
VIDAL SASSOON

Shampoo

Mmm . . . this has a nice pong — a bit like marzipan! It does the trick on the old hair too, leaving it soft 'n' sumptious (or something!). 4/5.

Mousse

Mmm . . . this has a nice pong . . . (OK! — The Ed.) It held my hair without being sticky — a good buy, I think! 4/5.

Hairspray

This is an ozone friendly, pump action production and cos I'm such a "green" chick, I love it! 5/5.

TESTING TESTING!

With the billions of different hair products available all claiming to do wonders for a boring barnet, how is a poor, bewildered young lass supposed to make up her mind? Well don't bother cos we'll do it for you! Here're our views on some of the very best and worst products on sale . . .

We go messing about on the river!

ON THE WATERFRONT

1

2

3

● 1. Cardigan, by Jeffrey Rogers at Top Shop. Shirt, by Kumar at Top Shop and C&A. Joggers, from Oasis. Commando Kickers, from Shelleys. Beads (courtesy of the Fashion Ed.!).

● 2. 3/4 length cardigan, from Top Shop. Crop sweat top, by Pamplemousse from Stirling Cooper. Skirt, by Phool (phone 01 568 6191 for stockists information). Necklace and belt, both by Pink Soda at Top Shop. Boots, from Shelleys. Tights, from The Sock Shop.

● 3. Aran jumper, (sold as part of set) by Kumar at Top Shop & C&A. Joggers, and shawl, both from Oasis. Chain belt, by Pink Soda at Top Shop. Necklace, by Baku at Etam. Boots (as before). Tights, from The Sock Shop.

● 4. Hooded sweat top, by Pamplemousse (phone 01 387 8797 for stockists). Shirt and skirt, both from Hennes. Scarf, by Phool (as before). Tights, (as before).

● 5. Cardigan, from Top Shop. Ruffle-neck blouse, by CCC at Top Shop. Embroidered skirt, from Hennes. Fringed scarf (around head), by Phool (as before). Tights, from The Sock Shop. Shoes, from Freeman Hardy Willis. Pendant necklace, by Pink Soda from Top Shop.

5 STAR

- COREY FELDMAN
- PATRICK DEMPSEY
- CHRISTIAN SLATER
- COREY HAIM
- JOHNNY DEPP

With the announcement of a new hunky film star every five minutes, it's difficult to keep track of the talent. We present you with five of our favourites, and we're sure you'll agree . . .

COREY FELDMAN

Six months before Mr Haim made his entrance into the world, his buddy Corey Feldman launched himself out into an unsuspecting hospital! During his early years, Corey's mum thrust him into the glare of showbiz, and by the age of three he was regularly appearing on commercials, sitcoms, and anything that required a sickeningly cute little boy! As well as starring in shows like 'Mork and Mindy', 'The Love Boat' and 'One Day At A Time', he appeared in some dodgy horror movies like 'The Body', 'Friday the 13th Parts 4 & 5' and 'Psycho 3'.

After this not-too-successful debut in the movie world, Corey finally struck gold, with four major hit films in three years. First came 'Gremlins' then 'Goonies', a teenage Indiana Jones type adventure yarn. 'Stand By Me' was a sensitive, classy and altogether tremendous look at teenage life in 1950's America, and starred Corey, Wil Wheaton and River Phoenix.

Possibly the jewel in Corey's crown is 'The Lost Boys', a film with absolutely everything! Everyone who's seen this film will be delighted to hear most of the cast have returned to film 'Lost Boys II'!

One of the most publicised parts of Corey Feldman's life is his friendship with Corey Haim, a story of romance, intrigue and wrecked hotel rooms! For a couple of years the Coreys were inseparable, but a much reported tiff led people to believe that Haim had stolen Feldman's girlfriend, which made him go out with Brigitte Neilsen on the rebound! The Coreys soon made up though, but before you could say "rawk and roll" they were hitting the scandal sheets again! Both Haim and Feldman went to Idaho to support a charity for Students Against Drunk Driving, and supposedly they trashed their hotel rooms so much that all money raised that night had to pay for the damage! Maybe these lads aren't as goody-goody as they look!

CONTINUED ▶

5 STAR

CHRISTIAN SLATER

Two years ago the response would have been "Christian who?" but today Mr Slater is one of the more popular young actors in the business. He was one of these lucky blighters who had parents in the acting business, but even if fate directed him to his profession, he's made the most of his chances!

At the age of 16 he won a major part in the Sean Connery film 'The Name Of The Rose', and all around the world critics sat up at the sight of this major new talent. At first Christian didn't fulfill his previous potential, but now he is off and running, and is definitely in the top five young actors league. After appearing as Jeff Bridges' son in 'Tucker', he won two major starring roles, which were released back-to-back. Firstly he played the rebellious character Brian Kelly in 'Gleaming The Cube'. He then played the murderously unhinged J.D. in many people's fave film of '89, 'Heathers'. Christian received rave reviews as this Jack Nicholson-style madman. Away from acting, Chrisian is a quiet, secretive person who is rumoured to be "dating" Winona Ryder who starred with him in 'Heathers'. Lucky Winona, eh girlies?!

PATRICK DEMPSEY

Patrick is one of the most down-to-earth and charming men on the movie circuit, and he's also one of the quietest.

At the age of 12 Patrick found out that he was dyslexic. He realised he was never going to become a hot-shot academic, so he decided to concentrate on his dramatic talents and at the age of 16 joined the Maine Acting Company. As well as acting, Patrick also mastered the fine arts of juggling and ventriloquism, which brought in a few dollars of pocket money won at talent shows and church concerts!

When Patrick made his move from theatre to TV, he won roles in a TV movie and the series of the film 'Fast Times At Ridgemont High', but he was just biding his time until something bigger and better came along, and pretty soon it did! Playing Ellsworth 'Sonny' Wisecarver, the 14-year-old romeo from the 1940's, brought him the fame he deserved in 'The Woo Woo Kid'. He soon followed this up with another romantic comedy, called 'Can't Buy Me Love'.

After these two rapid hits Patrick seemed to disappear but recently he's catapulted himself back into our hearts with two films showing him at his hilarious and lovable best. In 'Sisters' Pat goes to visit his Canadian girlfriend for Christmas, and before getting the big elbow he has to put up with the horrors of her family. In 'Loverboy' he plays a pizza delivery boy who often receives some rather over-friendly attention from some of his female customers!

COREY HAIM

Corey Ian Haim was born on December 23 1971 in Toronto, Canada. By all accounts Corey's childhood wasn't a very happy affair, and the more unhappy he became, the more trouble he got into! His one saving grace was his interest in acting, spurred on by big sister Carol. She introduced Corey to her acting classes, and soon enough he was signed up for a part in the Canadian TV series 'The Edison Twins'. A star was born!

After starring in this series for a while, Corey branched out into movies making 'Murphy's Romance', 'Silver Bullet' and 'Secret Admirer'. Although Corey was still based in Canada, when he won a role in American TV series 'Roomies', he had to move to Los Angeles. At the beginning of his time in California Corey felt extremely lonely. However, there was light at the end of the tunnel when he auditioned for a new movie. He met the director, won the role and gained the lead in 'The Lost Boys'! As well as launching his career as a fully-fledged star, it also introduced him to his best friend, Corey Feldman!

For the past couple of years Corey has been quite quiet on the film front, but he is just about to play the lead role in the movie 'The Amazing And Death-Defying Diary Of Eugene Dingham', where he plays a waiter, set in the 1950's. Look out for that one!

JOHNNY DEPP

He sports two mean tattoos, he plays in a rawk band and he rides a vintage Harley Davidson — is Johnny Depp the last original rebel? Well not when you realise one of his tattoos is a heart-shaped job in loving tribute to his mum Betty Sue, his fave hobby is making jewellery and he owns a pet turtle!

Born in Owensboro, Kentucky on June 9, 1963, John Christopher Depp was the youngest of four children. After a few years in the back woods of America, the Depp family moved to the more happenin' surroundings of Miramar, Florida, and it was there that Johnny was introduced to music. After getting to grips with his first $25 electric guitar, Johnny started to play in a few bands, and dropped out of school to move to Los Angeles with his band, Six Gun Method. After gaining a good live reputation, and even supporting Billy Idol, Six Gun Method waited for the inevitable record contract. And waited . . . and waited . . . Eventually Johnny realised this wasn't paying the rent, so went along to a movie audition as recommended by his acting buddy Nicolas Cage, and although he didn't have any acting experience he got the job. The role was of a young victim in a low budget horror film, but 'Nightmare On Elm Street' surprisingly made millions and launched both Freddy Kreuger and Johnny Depp!

After being savaged by the fingernails of Freddy Kreuger, he then played a minor part in the Oscar-winning Vietnam epic 'Platoon', but it was just after this when he won his star-making part in '21 Jump Street'. In this cop show with a twist, Johnny plays Tommy Hanson, a policeman who, along with his Jump Street mates, goes undercover in schools and colleges to solve teenage crimes.

At the moment Johnny isn't seriously romantically attached to anyone, and so far he hasn't exactly been lucky in love! He was married at 20 and divorced at 22, and last year he had a much publicised romance with 'Dirty Dancing' star Jennifer Grey, which again ended in tears! Poor wee soul!

10 REASONS WHY YOU CAN'T WITHOUT YER JA

Dear Mr/Mrs Newsagent,
Please reserve/deliver me one copy of the truly "wicked" and "happenin' " Jackie magazine each and every week.
Thanks a lot mate, yer a toff!

NAME: ____________

ADDRESS: ____________

1. The funkiest fashion pages in town!
2. Rather swoonsome posters!!
3. Brilliant beauty advice for foxy chicks near and far!
4. Lashings o' giveaways and competitions!
5. Our caring, sharing problem pages.
6. Lovey-dovey features on boys!
7. Soopah photo-stories!